SERVED BY LONDON'S TROLLEYBUSES

MICK WEBBER

SERVED BY LONDON'S TROLLEYBUSES

MICK WEBBER

Capital Transport

INTRODUCTION

The trolleybus played a vital, although relatively short-lived, role in the story of London's transport system. From its introduction in the 1930s as a new and exciting form of transport to Londoners, the trolleybus served the capital well until the early 1960s. It helped the population of London through the desperate times of the Second World War, and out into an austere peace and the rebuilding of the 1950s.

Trolleybuses had replaced the north London trams before the war, and but for the hostilities would have prevailed south of the river too. We can only imagine how the huge fleet would have fared had this occurred. The history of the vehicles has been admirably covered in depth in The London Trolleybus Volumes 1 and 2 by Ken Blacker, also published by Capital Transport, though Volume 2 is out of print and Volume 1 nearly so. The focus of this new book is principally on the routes and includes much new research.

The tram and trolleybus department had been a separate entity until it was merged with Central Buses in 1950, but even after this date it still seemed to keep its air of independence. The trolleybus fleet retained livery differences from the bus fleet, with the extra cream band and black lining out, until the end.

Thanks go to several people who have helped with this book. Tony Beard, Ken Blacker, Peter Carr, Keith Farrow, Jim Hawkins, Chris Holland, Peter Horner, Robin Newell and Antony Roskoss have all been very helpful, and Jim Whiting trawled the archives at TfL. I would also like to thank Robert Harley for his contribution to the pre-war chapter and Roy Makewell for his help with the South London Scheme and route details.

As always, photographers have been credited where possible, and my thanks go out to them for permission to reproduce their work. My sincere apologies go to anyone who has been missed.

Mick Webber

First published 2015

Published by Capital Transport Publishing Ltd
www.capitaltransport.com

Printed by Parksons Graphics

CONTENTS

Title page Leyland's photographer was out and about on 6th June 1936 to capture D1 class 384 as it came around the anti-clockwise loop at Dartford. The working was revised to work clockwise in August 1952. The vehicle had been delivered to London Transport in April 1936. *BCVM*

Above Numerically the first C1, Hounslow's No.132 heads a queue of trolleybuses at the stand by Shepherds Bush Green in summer 1950, not long after overhaul. *C Carter*

Left The road beneath the railway at Kingston Station was always susceptible to flooding. An extreme case is depicted here on 13th April 1937, when the water was deep enough for swimmers to brave it. *Topfoto*

TROLLEYBUSES FOR TRAMS

The formation on 1st July 1933 of the London Passenger Transport Board (LPTB) has been well documented. The new organisation inherited municipal tramways operated by the London County Council (LCC), West Ham, East Ham, Walthamstow, Ilford, Croydon, Erith and Bexley. Leyton Council Tramways had been operated by the LCC through a joint agreement. London United Tramways (LUT) and South Metropolitan Tramways & Lighting Company (SMET) were privately owned. The Metropolitan Electric Tramways (MET), serving routes from north London to the suburbs, was effectively a public/private venture in co-operation with the county councils of Middlesex and Hertfordshire. According to official sources the LPTB took possession of 2,630 trams operating over 328 route miles.

In addition to the railbound fleet, the LUT had already introduced the trolleybus to south west London from their Fulwell Depot. A total of 61 vehicles ran on four services initially: 1 Twickenham Junction to Tolworth; 2 Kingston Hill Loop to Tolworth; 3 The Dittons to Kingston Hill Loop; 4 Hampton Court to Wimbledon Station. These routes were introduced in May 1931, with route 5 following in 1932 as a Saturdays pm operation between Teddington and Malden. This limited operation route did not appear on maps. It did however, from 1935, get acknowledgement of its existence in the list of routes that appeared on the backs of the maps, but (by now numbered 605) just as a footnote to route 604. It later – extended to Wimbledon – became a frequent daily route. This chapter records the sequence of conversion from tram to trolleybus; more detailed information on dates will be found in the Depots and Their Routes chapter.

Trolleybus operation in London began on 16th May 1931 and London United Tramways' Fulwell depot was their first centre of operation, seen below with five vehicles of the original design in view. Services began on 16th May 1931. The inset shows the first routes as listed in a contemporary map.

The first London trolleybuses, operated by the London United Tramways, were very successful in drumming up trade and improving the LUT's finances. But, in mechanical and electrical terms they were by no means as successful as had been hoped, especially in terms of current consumption, and the bodywork caused serious problems. No.36 is seen in the early days on the Kingston loop route, and unusually does not show a route number on the blind. The upper front corner windows were later replaced with two panes of glass as body stress caused the curved glass to crack. *Mick Webber Collection*

Trolleybuses serving these seventeen route miles had proved to be a success. The new vehicles were popular and had generated increased revenue. The chairman of the LPTB, Sir Albert Stanley, Baron Ashfield of Southwell, was impressed by the financial results and by the favourable reaction of the travelling public. In its first thirteen months of tenure the new Board decided that the trolleybus was the way forward and prototype vehicles were ordered and tested. It was imperative that any tram replacement trolleybus could match as closely as possible the tramcar in passenger carrying ability.

A leading article in *The Transport World* for 13th December 1934 described the search for a high capacity trolleybus: 'For some time past the Board has been experimenting with two or three types of vehicles for the new trolleybus routes. One has a standard AEC 663T six-wheel chassis, with a wheelbase increased to 18ft 7in, making the overall length 29ft 11in. It has seats for 73 passengers, the body being by Metropolitan-Cammell-Weymann, and the electrical equipment by Metropolitan-Vickers. The second vehicle has a standard AEC 661T chassis, with a wheelbase of 16ft 3in and an overall length of 25ft 11in. The four-wheeler has 60 seats, and both body and electrical equipment are by the English Electric Company. The bodies are all-metal, and both units are driven by self-ventilating compound motors, provided with special winding to give improved motor characteristics with regenerative control. Each has made a total of about 10,000 miles in experimental runs.'

In fact, two prototypes (62–63) were trialled by the LPTB for the coming fleet and the design chosen was the six-wheeled vehicle, No. 62. While these tests were taking place, little time was lost in preparing Parliamentary legislation for the change from trams to trolleybuses. The 1933 LPTB Act had already granted the Board powers to abandon any tramway route, provided three months notice was given to the relevant highway authorities. Further powers were gained on 31st July 1934, when the Royal Assent was given to a Bill for services in the west London, Middlesex, north Kent and Croydon areas to be converted to the newer form of electric traction. Thereafter, successive Bills paved the way in the mid and late 1930s for what was to become the world's largest trolleybus network. In the first two years of its existence the LPTB was not committed to the total eradication of the tramcar on London's streets. Board officials stated in front of Parliamentary Select Committees that trunk tramway routes would be retained for 'the foreseeable future'.

However, this policy of tramway retention soon withered on the vine. There was a strong anti-tram lobby, which included politicians, commercial interests and motoring organisations. The Publicity department at London Transport was early into the field of promoting the trolleybus. Aside from employing the staff magazine *Pennyfare* as their mouthpiece, they briefed local newspapers and professional and trade publications such as *The Commercial Motor* and *The Transport World*. The emphasis was always on the modernity of the new vehicles.

London Transport's first trolleybuses were indeed a big step up from the Diddlers, and the assembled press and dignitaries were treated to a preview and trial run. A journalist from the Brentford and Chiswick times reported:

'Many curious and speculative eyes were focused on a strange, but most imposing vehicle which passed through the borough on Tuesday morning. Rather like a super luxury omnibus, with beautifully upholstered seats, it was driven through the main streets with smooth noiseless motion, as it passed with exquisite ease through the maze of traffic, and its bright spick and span appearance attracted immediate attention. The new modernist vehicle was the first of the trolley omnibus service, which is to replace the trams. On Tuesday, the experimental run commenced from Fulwell, and the route followed was through Twickenham, Busch Corner, Brentford, Kew, Young's Corner to Hammersmith, then back to Young's Corner, and thence to Shepherds Bush. The return journey made the same route, and ended in Hounslow in the afternoon.' As the service commenced on Sunday 27th October 1935, it would appear that this trip took place on Tuesday 22nd.

BIRMINGHAM
RAILWAY CARRIAGE & WAGON CO., LTD.,
SMETHWICK

Pioneers in the construction of Steel Passenger Stock. Specialists in the designing and building of all types of Coaches for Steam or Electric Traction; Diesel, Petrol or Steam driven Rail Cars; Air-Conditioned Cars, Tramcar Bodies, Omnibus Bodies, High Capacity Wagons and Freight Cars of every description; Containers, etc.

Telephone No.: Smethwick 1294.

Telegrams: "Carriage, Smethwick."

On and from October 27, Trolleybuses will be substituted for trams on routes as shown below:

Tram Route		Trolleybus Route	
ROUTE	SECTION BETWEEN		
26	Hammersmith and Kew Bridge	667	Hammersmith and Hampton Court every 3 minutes to Kew Bridge every 6 minutes to Hampton Court
67	Hammersmith and Hampton Court		
57	Shepherds Bush and Hounslow The Bell	657	Shepherds Bush and Hounslow (Wellington Road) every 4 minutes
63	Shepherds Bush and Kew Bridge		

Certain early and late journeys between Young's Corner and Hammersmith Broadway now operated by route 26 will not be continued by the Trolleybuses.

TIMES of first and last Trolleybuses are shown overleaf.

Brand new C2 class No.198 stands resplendent in the sunshine at Hammersmith on route 667 in the spring of 1936. Two other service trolleybuses are behind, with a third in the background blinded up as 'Special'. *W J Haynes*

Both front screens are open on what appears to be a warm summer day. 132 was numerically the first of the C1 class, and was delivered in October 1935. It is shown here at Kew Bridge with a healthy load, and alongside the bus stop is a feeder pillar and some typical LPTB enamel signage. *G H F Atkins*

The first major act in the conversion programme occurred on 27th October 1935, when route 657 was inaugurated from Hounslow to Shepherds Bush, with Hounslow Depot supplying the vehicles. At the same time Fulwell Depot saw its last tramcar, as route 667 took to the road from Hampton Court to Hammersmith. It became standard practice for trolleybus routes to be numbered in the 600s and, from March 1938, 500s also; the existing Kingston services also fell into line with this scheme. With tram services having been taken over by the LPTB from a number of undertakings, there were many cases of duplicated route numbers. For example, while the Hounslow tram service 57 became trolleybus 657, the Chingford Mount 57 was to become 557.

Opposite Two of the B2 class are crossing Beresford Square in Woolwich, making their way to the terminus at the Free Ferry. The blinds of both 100 and 103 have already been turned for the return journeys. These short-wheelbase 60 seaters were already proving inadequate for these routes, and would soon be replaced by newer 70-seat vehicles. The date is 28th February 1936. *BCVM*

After Fulwell and Hounslow, attention then switched the following month to the tramways of the former Bexley and Erith undertakings, where the track was in a very poor state. Route 698 replaced trams from Bexleyheath to Abbey Wood and was extended beyond the latter terminus to Woolwich Ferry at the same time. Over this section trams on services 36 and 38 continued to run, thus preserving access to Abbey Wood Depot. Later in November, the main trunk route 696 was inaugurated between Woolwich and Dartford, Market Street. A purpose built trolleybus depot at Bexleyheath was constructed for routes 696 and 698, as none of the former council-owned tramway buildings were deemed suitable for conversion.

The long suffering passengers in Croydon, obliged to sit on wooden seats on open top tramcars, were treated to an enhanced standard of comfort when route 654 made the connection between Sutton, West Croydon and Crystal Palace. This conversion was effected in two stages, in December 1935 and February 1936. In fact the next ten months of 1936 saw an accelerating programme of tram replacements, as swathes of the old LUT and MET systems fell to the latest form of electric traction. In April, route 660 replaced trams from Hammersmith to Acton. This was but a prelude to the establishment of a longer through service, numbered 666, which commenced operation in July between Hammersmith and Edgware. Route 660 reappeared in a slightly different form in August, when on Mons-Sats it linked North Finchley and Hammersmith. At the same time route 645 began from Edgware to North Finchley.

The B1 class were equipped with coasting and run-back brakes suitable for the steep Anerley Hill, and operated route 654 throughout its life. Leyland's official photographer caught No.89 as it offloads passengers on arrival at Crystal Palace on 28th February 1936, soon after introduction. *BCVM*

C3 class No.334 was not very old when this view was taken on route 660 at Willesden Junction. It had been delivered in July 1936, and the weather looks to be very warm as most of the windows are open. The route was introduced to run from North Finchley to Hammersmith in August of 1936. *Bus of Yesteryear*

Though not built exclusively for trolleybuses, this new roundabout at Hampton Court was ideal for trolleybuses terminating on routes 604 and 667 to turn round. The photographer has probably waited for one of the new vehicles on the 667 to make its turn before taking his picture. *London Transport Museum*

The summer of 1936 saw another inauguration of trolleybuses when, in August, route 662 began operating from Sudbury to Paddington, where it terminated in company with the new 664 from Paddington to Edgware. The last months of the year witnessed the trolleybus making three further inroads into tramway territory. Two months later, the new vehicles crossed the River Lea into Essex for the first time, as route 623 linked Woodford with Manor House in north London. Back in the former London United domain former trunk tram route 7 between Uxbridge and Shepherds Bush fell victim to the 607 in mid-November. The final trolleybus nail in the LUT coffin occurred four weeks later, when tram route 55 from Hanwell to Brentford was replaced by trolleybuses on service 655.

All appeared set fair for a complete abandonment of the tram system. In 1937, Parliamentary legislation was obtained for this purpose and it was predicted that the last of the railbound vehicles would vanish from the streets of the capital in 1942. The staff magazine *Pennyfare* was quick to toe the party line in its March issue: 'This year Parliament will be invited to assent to the introduction of trolleybuses on the remaining 148 miles of tramways under the control of the Board. The cost of this large conversion will, it is estimated, amount to some £10,000,000.'

Clearly, the LPTB had been given the green light by the Treasury to finish the job. However, the best laid plans of Lord Ashfield and the LPTB were coming under increased scrutiny. Trolleybuses were not everybody's cup of tea. The appearance of poles and overhead wires in locations served by conduit equipped tramways caused some protest from environmentalists. At sensitive places such as Westminster Bridge and the Victoria Embankment there was a veritable storm of objections to the idea of 'festoons of overhead cables'.

The twenty-five vehicles of the E3 class were AECs with Park Royal bodywork. Numerically the first, No.629, was also the first to be delivered in February 1937. It has been moved into the open by the Park Royal tractor and stands behind East Kent JG 8237, which was a Leyland TD4. The trolleybus has yet to have its poles, number plates and wheel trims added. The body was destroyed in a raid at West Ham in 1944 and the vehicle was subsequently rebodied. Apart from the rebodied examples, all of the class was withdrawn by the end of 1956.

Sir George Hume, MP for Greenwich, raised another issue of the supposed negative effect of trolleybuses, when he spoke in the House of Commons on 26th July 1937 about the turning circle needed for an extended 698 to Eltham:

Sir G. Hume asked the Minister of Transport whether he is aware that, pursuant to the powers given under the London Passenger Transport Board Act, 1937, it is proposed to provide a service of trolleybuses along the residential road known as Sherard Road, Eltham, and that this road is 21 feet wide at its narrowest; that the trolleybuses will be superimposed on four services of omnibuses already using the road, and that there is a strong opinion in Eltham generally against the use of Sherard Road either for omnibuses or trolleybuses, because it is considered to be unsuitable and dangerous for such traffic.

In this case, since the legislation had already been enacted, the Minister, Mr Burgin, regretted he could do nothing to assuage the householders of Eltham. The use of residential streets, be it in the centre of town or out in the suburbs, for trolleybus terminal loops, continued to generate opposition, a subject we return to later in this chapter.

Among plans aborted for other reasons were for a 624 trolleybus between Tottenham Hale and Manor House and a 639 between Winchmore Hill and Muswell Hill to replace the 39A tram and a 673 between Wanstead Flats and Royal Albert Dock to replace the 73 tram. A few trolleybus traction poles had already been erected at the southern end of the 73 tram route. At one stage the 623 was to have continued beyond Manor House to Tottenham Court Road and, at another, a 671 would have taken over most of the 71 tram service which was later absorbed into the new 679.

The Board was always keen to experiment, and in 1936 work began on a new trolleybus with a front exit which would have doors controlled by the driver. It was to be of chassisless construction and the body was to be built at Charlton Works. The vehicle became X4 class No.754. This view shows the vehicle after it had been partly panelled. The work was completed, and the vehicle handed over on 1st March 1937. It worked its whole life from Finchley Depot. *LT Museum*

The emphasis in 1937 was on Metropolitan Essex and the extensive tramway network that existed in the East End. All the back street tram routes would be swept away in four stages. First up in January, the Walthamstow area saw the opening of route 685 from Markhouse Road to the Crooked Billet. This was followed in June by the introduction of routes 687, 697 and 699, which pursued different routeings in their journeys from Chingford Mount to the Victoria and Albert Docks. Completing the set of new services was route 669 from Stratford Broadway to Canning Town.

The turn of West Ham and East Ham came in September and October 1937, when the Stratford and East Ham circular services 689 and 690 were inaugurated and route 685 was extended to Canning Town. The Ilford area was tackled on 6th February 1938, when route 691 commenced operation from Barking to Barkingside; it was joined by the 693 from Chadwell Heath to Barking, and on 12th February by the short lived 692 from Newbury Park to Chadwell Heath. Route 669 was also extended over previously tramless streets to a terminus adjacent to the northern pier of the Woolwich Ferry.

It is 6th June 1937, and trolleybus 622 has been chosen to make a ceremonial run from West Ham depot to the Greengate. It arrives with the Mayor Mrs Daisy Parsons at the wheel and an official also in the cab to keep an eye on the proceedings. Apparently, it was driven on batteries but with the poles up on the wires. A plaque commemorating the event was fixed to the lower deck bulkhead, and remained on the vehicle through its operating life. It also closed operations in April 1960. *Topfoto*

Route 692 was introduced on 12th February 1938 running on Saturday afternoons and evenings. It lasted only until 3rd December 1938, when it was withdrawn. E1 587 is seen at Newbury Park. *Charles Klapper*

The Docks routes began on 6th June 1937, and the 697 linked them with Chingford Mount. E3 652 had arrived in the same month, and is pictured at Stratford. The Park Royal bodies on these AECs were not as durable as most, and were withdrawn earlier than the other E classes. They were easily recognisable by the four pairs of vents at the front between decks. *LT Museum*

The narrow East End streets, once the territory of Corporation trams, now have new servants. C3 class 339 pauses on route 697. There is no stop here, so perhaps the inspector on the pavement has requested the driver to pull in. The Metropolitan stage carriage plate 5916 is clearly visible above the used ticket box release hatch. A Bedford delivery van is parked opposite and the advert hoarding on the left shows just how things can change over the years, with coal going from hero to villain. What did make London clean, of course, were the trolleybuses. The date is 24th February 1939.
LT Museum

Next spread As first constructed for trolleybuses, overhead provision was additionally made at Greengate junction, West Ham, for tram operation and accounts for the additional east/west running wires. In the early days of trolleybuses, only heavy wood-framed insulation was commercially available for special work fittings, as illustrated by this view. A lighter, more visually acceptable type of 'dumbell' insulation was later adopted by LT, though wood framed special work remained in use at this junction until the end of operations. Of particular interest is the centre wire arrangement whereby trolleybuses running to and from the depot were required to swing trolley poles. The tram wires were removed with the conversion of the London to Barking route in June 1940, but the centre wire arrangement for trolleybuses lasted another year. It was difficult to operate in the blackout conditions of wartime, and was replaced by a more conventional arrangement in the summer of 1941.
LT Museum

Although the focus of attention had been on the East End, there was one important conversion on 12th September 1937 in the western area of the capital. Vehicles on route 630 made the long trek from West Croydon to terminate at the junction of Harrow Road and Scrubs Lane. Also introduced at this stage were the 612 from Battersea Princes Head to Mitcham Fair Green, the peak hours only 626 from Clapham Junction to Acton and the 628 from Clapham Junction to Craven Park. This conversion was notable in that for the first time trolleybuses replaced trams working over conduit tracks, doing so on the section from Putney Bridge Road to Tooting Junction.

Wandsworth depot operated both trams and trolleybuses, route 612 starting on 12th September 1937. The planned eventual conversion to all trolleybus operation never materialised. D3 512 is shown here passing E3 class tram 1908 on route 31.
Mick Webber Collection

Falcon Road is the setting as D2 402 on the 628 leads F1 657 on the 655 away from the terminus in Grant Road near Clapham Junction station. The 628 had started on 12th September 1937 and the 655 the previous December.
John Aldridge Collection

The main thrust of 1938 involved the wholesale abandonment of former MET tram routes linking central London termini with the suburbs in Middlesex and Hertfordshire. There was plenty of work for construction crews, who had to instal overhead equipment – poles and wires – where none had previously existed due to the presence of tramways worked on the conduit system within the LCC area. In March, the completion of new wiring which joined the former tram termini of Grays Inn Road and Farringdon Road, enabled paired trolleybus routes to operate round the Holborn loop. Taking advantage of this facility were services 517/617 and 521/621. The former linked North Finchley to Holborn via Highgate; the latter served the same termini, but went via Wood Green. Also making an appearance was route 609 from Barnet to Moorgate, Finsbury Square, and the short-lived 651 from Barnet to Cricklewood.

The 651 was not only short-lived but a late addition to the plans. A document dated 30th June 1936 does not include it and shows a number of variations from what was actually introduced at this time. Tram route 19 (Barnet to Tottenham Court Road) was to have been replaced in March 1938 by a trolleybus route numbered 619 with the 645 extended from Finchley to Whetstone. Among other variations from what eventually occurred to appear in the same document were tram routes 3 (Hampstead Heath and Holborn) and 5 (Hampstead Heath and Moorgate) being replaced by new routes 606 and 608; these were to run from Hampstead depot, which in the event never operated trolleybuses and was closed with the end of trams. Hampstead depot was also listed to accommodate the replacements for tram routes 7 (Parliament Hill Fields and Holborn) and 15 (Parliament Hill Fields and Moorgate), the former taking the route number 610. The plan covered the two years until 30th June 1938 only and so not all north London routes were included. There were no 500-series routes listed, but by the end of 1937 it had been decided to use this series of numbers also. The first planned use of such a number appears to have been 537. By this time the trolleybus replacement for tram route 3 had become 637, and 537 was planned for use when it was decided to run the route both ways around the Holborn loop. It is interesting to note that even with the south London routes added, there would never have been more than 95 trolleybus routes, but the use of a batch of 200 possibilities enabled more trolleybus route numbers to have some likeness to the tram service numbers they replaced. With most this was achieved.

On 8th May, route 629 was inaugurated between Enfield and Tottenham Court Road. Route 641 replaced trams on the Winchmore Hill to Moorgate service and route 625 forged another link between Middlesex and Essex, when it began operation between Wood Green and Woodford. The fate of the Hampstead group of tram routes was sealed in July with the introduction of the 513/613 from Hampstead and Parliament Hill Fields to the Holborn loop, the 615 from Parliament Hill Fields to Moorgate and the 639 from Hampstead Heath to Moorgate.

The pace of the conversions now increased with two stages in quick succession. In mid-October 1938, trolleybuses inaugurated three major trunk services. The 649 ran from Stamford Hill to Ponders End; the 659 forged a link from Waltham Cross in Hertfordshire to Holborn Circus; the 679 linked Waltham Cross with Smithfield. Less than a month later, route 627 commenced from Tottenham Court Road to Edmonton. Fears were expressed at this time that the supply of vehicles was being stretched to the limit. Both AEC and Leyland Motors were working hard to keep up with demand. Coupled with this, concerns were voiced that perfectly serviceable ex MET tramcars were being sacrificed and sent for scrap unnecessarily.

Route 639, along with the other Hampstead routes, commenced operation on 10th July 1938, replacing trams from Hampstead depot. Holloway was the operating base, and short wheelbase B1 class No.491 is seen on the 639 at Moorgate, Finsbury Square. *Don Thompson*

Over a five-year period from 1935 to 1940, around 1,650 trolleybuses were built for service in London. In this view of the Leyland body shop in October 1938 work is under way on the 300-strong K class of trolleybuses. Three upper and one lower deck can be seen; the one nearest the camera has yet to be panelled. *BCVM*

Even though the clouds of war were gathering, the hectic pace of getting rid of London's trams showed no sign of letting up. In February 1939, the 649 was extended from Stamford Hill to Liverpool Street Station and new route 643 linked Wood Green to Holborn Circus. Stamford Hill was the terminus of the new 647 to London Docks and the 683 to Moorgate. The circuitous tram route 53 from Aldgate to Tottenham Court Road succumbed to trolleybus route 653 four weeks later. With this stage north London had been effectively cleared of almost all its trams, except for Highgate Hill route 11 and the Kingsway Subway services 31, 33 and 35. The east London trunk routes still operated, but plans were in hand to do away with them as soon as possible.

The K class all Leyland vehicles were the largest single class of trolleybuses delivered to London Transport. K2 No.1155 is pictured at Stamford Hill about to terminate – the driver has already changed the blind for the return journey. *Charles Klapper*

In the case of the Kingsway Subway a prototype trolleybus was constructed, but progress was limited and a number of problems needed to be ironed out before tramcars could be evicted from their subterranean dwelling. As events turned out, the rebuilding to suit trackless vehicles was postponed indefinitely and the three Kingsway Subway tram routes would survive into the post war era. The special Subway trolleybus 1379 did a run through it on 13th August 1939. Among the plans for the subway had been the installation of a turntable at the south end.

The final steps were now being taken to render the East End a tram free zone. On 11th June, Bloomsbury received service 555 to Leyton Green and service 581 to Woodford. The 649 at Liverpool Street was joined by the 557 to Chingford Mount. Thus, the final peacetime conversion passed off with very little incident.

An important task in the conversion of tram routes to trolleybuses was that of finding suitable turning circles for the new vehicles. In a number of cases the depots could be used if they were conveniently located at the end of a route (as was the case with Lea Bridge) or at a point where a short-working facility was needed. In a few other cases, such as at Uxbridge, Woodford, Highgate Village and Hounslow, special turning facilities were constructed. Most new turning circles however used existing street layouts and in some cases, these proved difficult to get approval for, both in central London and in the suburbs, where residents were unhappy about the new vehicles parking in their streets.

In the north London scheme, Frank Pick is known to have had ambitions to get trolleybuses on at least some of the tram routes terminating at Tottenham Court Road to continue south and turn in Trafalgar Square, but this was not to be. Then three options needed to be looked at for trolleybuses to turn at in the Tottenham Court Road area, first one using Bedford Square, and then one via Francis Street and finally the adopted loop via Howland Street and Maple Street. At Holborn the lack of an acceptable turning circle resulted in a large loop working between there and King's Cross. Aldersgate also lacked any turning facilities, so the service to the top of Aldersgate Street was lost when the terminus moved to Smithfield via Clerkenwell Road.

In planning the south London scheme, there were more complications. The largest of these was in respect of the tram services around the Victoria Embankment, where Westminster City Council's strong resistance to trolleybus overhead on Westminster Bridge had not been overcome by the start of the war. Strong, and successful, resistance to having trolleybuses turn in the vicinity of King's Road, Chelsea led to two alternative loops (Danvers Street and Paulton Square or Fulham Road, Callow Street and Elm Park Road) failing to get approval and the consequent truncation of the planned tram route 34 trolleybus replacement at Clapham Junction with a planned extension of bus route 31 instead. At Victoria, two loops were proposed, one via Wilton Road and Gillingham Street and a second via Gillingham Street and Warwick Street.

Services to another Thames bridge causing concern were those tram services terminating on the north side of Southwark Bridge. There were clearly problems in finding a turning facility north of the bridge as two options were looked at south of the bridge; either using Thrale Street or Union Street. Both plans were dropped following police objections to trolleybuses turning into Southwark Street at these two points. Another proposal put forward by the Board for this terminus was for a loop working by which trolleybuses would continue beyond the tram terminus via Queen Victoria Street, King William Street and Cannon Street to return to Southwark Bridge. Replies to another proposal imply that another option suggested was to run via Cannon Street and London Bridge to form a loop. The City authorities objected to these proposals owing to the increase in traffic they would generate along these thoroughfares. The two termini each side of London Bridge station, one in Tooley Street for what was to become the 570 and one in Southwark Street for the 612 and 626 extensions, would have been connected by wiring under the LPTB 1937 bill, but this also was thrown out owing to concerns about the increased congestion it was felt would be caused in Borough High Street. Within a few years, the work done on planning for trolleybuses in south London was in any case to become largely wasted, though some of the turning circles in south London were in due course adopted for the bus services that took over from trams in post-war London.

Opposite Hackney depot is well on the way to becoming a trolleybus depot. Officials stand and watch as the assembled workers remove the tram lines in preparation for the new intake of K class trolleybuses, one of which can be seen in the background. Routes 555, 581 and 677 were to work from here. *LT Museum*

As the inevitable war with Germany approached, thousands of children were evacuated from the capital, and some trolleybuses were used to ferry them to railway stations. D3 class No.535 is employed on this task as the children patiently queue with their gas masks at hand.
Mick Webber Collection

After war was declared in the first week of September 1939, the blackout was rigidly enforced and this effectively put the damper on any 'last tram celebrations' when, on 5th November, the changeover of electric traction modes took place at Aldgate, as trolleybus routes 661 and 663, to Leyton and Ilford respectively, began their careers. Previous to this, tram route 77 had vacated Aldersgate in order to give way to trolleybuses one week after the declaration of war. The replacing 677 vehicles were obliged to turn round at Smithfield, and delays had also been caused at the other end of the route by the inability of the Board to find and construct a suitable turning site at the West India Docks terminus.

A similar problem had arisen in Highgate Village, where some haggling had been going on for a number of months as to the position of the turning loop for trolleybus route 611. Eventually, compensation was paid to property owners and several buildings had to be demolished. The whole matter was sorted out by 10th December, when tram route 11 from Moorgate breathed its last. After the tracks on Highgate Hill fell silent, there remained only the trunk routes from Barking to Aldgate and Bloomsbury, which were serviced by depots at Poplar and West Ham. The end for east London's trams came on 10th June 1940, when route 565 was inaugurated from Holborn Circus to East Ham Town Hall; it was joined by the 567 from Aldgate to West Ham and by the 665 from Bloomsbury to Barking.

An article published in the July issue of *Pennyfare* included some interesting facts and figures:

130 trams of routes 65 and 67 were put into store, 147 new trolleybuses stole over their road – creatures of startling quiet in the clamour of Poplar. It meant – this swapping of horses, this silent revolution – training 250 tram crews, average age 40, for nine days; putting up 660 steel poles, 28 miles of wire; enlarging Poplar Depot half

War had been declared on Sunday 3rd September 1939 and route 677 was new in the coming week. K2 No.1318 and K1 No.1070 are showing their new white mudguards and lamp masking in preparation for the blackout.
Charles Klapper

as much again and rebuilding the old part, adapting West Ham Depot as well; clearing one part of Poplar Depot at a time to take up rails, lay a new, smooth floor, and put down temporary rails; on the first day, pulling up temporary rails and laying timber over inspection pits, while trolleybuses kept coming in – 100 of them in Poplar alone. For all those who collect statistics: today 256 miles of trolleybus route, 102 miles of tram route: north of the Thames the only trams are those on the Embankment and Kingsway routes. Trolleybuses number 1,671; trams 1,127.

Thus the 'silent revolution' came to an end. Officially the abandonment of the south London tramways was put on hold for the duration of the war; however, there were straws in the wind concerning the viability of the trolleybus. Advances in motor bus design and technology, particularly in regards to the development of the diesel engine, had not gone unnoticed by the LPTB. On 12th February 1937, *The Commercial Motor* published a leading article entitled *Is the Trolleybus a Passing Phase?* The reporter had been briefed by a London Transport official, conceivably someone close to Deputy Chairman, Frank Pick, who was always a sceptic when it came to the replacement of trams by trolleybuses. The article contained the statement: 'all things being equal, there is little doubt that the Board would have decided to add oil engined buses to its present fleet to make up for the loss of the trams..'. Obviously, there were those in the LPTB who were unconvinced of the merits of the trolleybus. One of the major arguments for the continuance of electric traction was that the infrastructure – feeder cables, substations etc – was already in place and would be wasted by a straight conversion from tram to bus. This approach had appealed to Lord Ashfield, but the voices of the pro-bus lobby were gaining in influence and were going to be heard loud and clear after the Second World War was over.

The tram to trolleybus conversions, as we have already seen, continued into the War, and the north London trams had all but been mopped up by the new vehicles by the time the programme came to a halt on 9th June 1940, when Poplar was converted. Nothing much changed during the early months of war, a period known as the "phoney war". September 1940 saw the beginning of deliveries of fifty new trolleybuses of the K3 and P1 classes, which took a year to complete.

The bombing, when it came, caused extensive disruptions to the trolleybus network and the linesmen and maintenance crews faced considerable challenges to keep the services operating under extreme conditions. There follow a few examples which involved diversion of trolleybuses or temporary replacement by buses. On the 15th and 16th October 1940, damage to the feeder cables in Worple Road resulted in the service between Kingston and Wimbledon being replaced by buses, and on the same night, the Tolworth loop was out of action due to a crater. On 1st November, a delayed action bomb in Lower Road Belvedere closed the road between Manor Way and Crabtree Manor Way, with trolleybuses turning either side. In the same area, on November 15th, a landmine in Erith Road Barnehurst, caused route 698 to be terminated at Brook Street, with buses covering the rest of the route.

L3 class No.1525 negotiates Gardiners Corner on route 665 showing its full wartime additions. White mudguards, headlamp masks and window netting have all been applied and the clippie stands on the platform whilst a 661 waits in the Whitechapel Road.
LT Museum

The very harsh reality of war. K1 1128 was left in this state after major blast damage in Stoke Newington on 18th September 1940. The vehicle was rebodied in 1942. *LT Museum*

Below Most damage to vehicles was inflicted by blast, and in one such incident, L3 No.1439 has had all of its windows blown in or broken. It is the subject of much scrutiny as it stands outside the Methodist Chapel in Benledi Street, Poplar on 10th December 1940. *Mick Webber Collection*

The first depot to be seriously affected by bombing was Bexleyheath. Severe blast damage was sustained when the depot was hit on 7th November 1940. Four trolleybuses had their bodies destroyed, B2 No.95, D2 No.406 and H1s 792 and 795 all being rebodied by Weymann in 1941/2. Many others suffered blast damage, and much of the depot structure had to be repaired.

On routes 612 and 630, a side street diversion was wired to avoid a large crater in Garratt Lane on 22nd February 1941 for two days, although the damage report does not state the roads used. Reports are also vague about the disruption caused between 8th and 10th March 1941, when trolleybuses were diverted at Plaistow High Street to avoid an unsafe water conduit. On the same date, the Holborn loop was closed due to an unexploded bomb. The clockwise loop was diverted along Clerkenwell Road and the anti-clockwise route used a temporarily wired Mount Pleasant. A major incident occurred on 20th April 1941, when the current from Greenwich power station was cut off in the Commercial Road. Some power was restored when two of the substations had special connections made to railway substations. When the power situation was rectified, a 500 yard diversion down New Road had to be wired to avoid the crater.

K1 class No. 1123 had its body written off after an incident at Dalston on 8th November 1940, the day after Bexleyheath depot was hit. The severity of the blast can be clearly seen here as it stands in Stamford Hill depot awaiting assessment. Its new body was supplied in December 1941.
LT Museum

H1 class No.790 is waiting at the stop near Plumstead Station bound for Dartford on 28th April 1942. Special shelters were provided here for the many workers employed at Woolwich Arsenal. This trolleybus later had its body completely destroyed at Bexleyheath, when the depot was hit by a flying bomb on 29th June 1944, and was rebodied by East Lancs in August 1946. *LT Museum*

On 19th April 1941, the road at Leman Street was completely blocked by debris, and route 647 was diverted to turn at Liverpool Street until 13th May. Routes 693 and 695 were not operating between Green Lanes and Chadwell Heath on 12th March 1943 due to another unexploded bomb, and buses were used to fill the gap. Putney High Street suffered considerable damage on 8th November due to a high explosive bomb, and trolleybuses worked single line around the obstruction.

The service on routes 657 and 667 was affected on 24th February 1944, when an unexploded bomb caused closure between Busch Corner and Brentford Half Acre. Buses ran as replacements working via the Great West Road. A damaged bridge at Grove Road, Bethnal Green, caused trolleybuses to be turned either side, and four days later, damage to the overhead at St Johns Hill, Battersea forced vehicles to turn each side of the obstacle. Blast damage at North Woolwich on 6th July caused two railway trucks to be blown into the road along with substantial debris, and consequently routes 569, 669 and 685 were reversing at Clyde Road. The 654 was affected on the 11th when a V1 brought down four bays of wires, and trolleybuses were turned at Thicket Road.

Towards the end of the year, another diversion was necessary in the East End, when wires were brought down at the junction of Argyle Road and Prince Regents Lane on 29th December. The Prince Regents Lane service was diverted via Balaam Street, New Barn Street and Freemasons Road.

Substantial damage to wiring and the roadway in Green Street on 26th January 1945 enforced a diversion. Poles were planted and wiring erected along Stukeley Road and Boleyn Road to avoid the incident. The crews worked through very difficult conditions to reinstate the services. Another incident in Chingford Mount Road on 7th February brought down three bays of overhead and the service between Crooked Billett and Chingford Mount was covered by buses.

It should be underlined that this is only a small sample of the many huge problems that were inflicted on the system during the hostilities, and the public were very rarely without a service in some form or another.

The losses to the fleet were beginning to be felt and an appeal was made to provincial operators for help. The help accepted came from Bournemouth Corporation in the shape of 18 twin-staircase dual doorway Sunbeams. They arrived in December 1940 and, as they required more headroom than London trolleybuses, were sent to Ilford depot because of the absence of bridges on the local routes. The front exit doors were not used in London service. After deliveries of the SA class began, the Bournemouth trolleybuses were no longer needed. Nine returned home in November 1941 and the other nine moved on to help out in Newcastle in September 1942.

The next major incident involving loss of vehicles occurred on 9th March 1941. This time West Ham depot was the casualty, and the major victims were H1 803 and K2 1247, which had their bodies destroyed, and chassisless L3 class 1492, which was destroyed completely. This was the first trolleybus to be written off. Before the dust had settled on this event, on the 19th, two other trolleybuses had their bodies destroyed. E2 621 was working from West Ham in Plaistow Road when it was hit, and N1 1587 from Bow was a casualty in a separate event. To illustrate the nightmares inflicted on the operating of services during this period, the list of events in just one 12-hour period occurring from 6pm on Wednesday 19th March until 6am on 20th March also included the following:

Highgate substation damaged by blast.
Charlton Works damaged by incendiary bombs.
Poplar depot foreman stores burnt out; side wall of depot damaged.
Bow depot roofing damaged by blast.
Hackney depot blast damage, and wires down in Bohemia Place.
West Ham depot roof damaged by blast.
Limehouse substation blast damage.
Silvertown Station, trolleybus damaged by blast.
Stratford Broadway trolleybus cash office damaged.
Silvertown Way, trolleybus damaged by blast.
Benson Road, Bexley, trolleybus damaged by blast.
Overhead wires down in Warton Street, Stratford,
Canning Town Station.
Aberfeldy Street Poplar.
Woodgrange Park, Romford Road.
Lea Bridge Station.

Eighteen Bournemouth trolleybuses arrived in London on loan in December 1940. No.145 was a Sunbeam/Park Royal vehicle built in 1935, and is working on the 691. The rear view shows No.77 in Barking with a wartime painted bus shelter in the foreground. Nine of the vehicles were returned to the south coast in November 1941 and the others, including No.145, were towed up to Newcastle where they helped out until 1945. *LT Museum*

Opposite top Bow depot on 26th September 1940. Structural damage has been suffered and N1 1622 has been affected along with a few others. New panels and glass would soon be fitted, and the travelling public would probably not even be aware of the work needed to keep the service running. *LT Museum*

Opposite bottom D3 class trolleybus 530 is being used here to demonstrate the virtues of the protective wire netting which was glued to the window glass. The bodywork has not suffered much damage beyond having a number of windows blown in, but there is a dent visible in the rear lower panel. *LT Museum*

On 11th March 1941, a memo from the General Manager was sent to the Chairman. It raised the subject of some new trolleybuses due to be delivered to South African operators. The delivery had been suspended due to shipping restrictions, and the memo went on to suggest that the Board should seek permission to hire these vehicles. It was pointed out that "three more trolleybuses were destroyed last night at West Ham" and that the Board would be wise to seek out any vehicles that it could find. The question of the eight-feet wide restriction was raised, and it was thought that the Ministry of Transport might waive the regulations, subject to reasonable terms. In a subsequent meeting on the 20th, this suggestion was agreed. The South African operators were approached about this possible loan, but were reluctant to accept, not being willing to take a chance on what condition the vehicles would be in once London had finished with them. In the end, the Board agreed to negotiate a purchase price for the trolleybuses, and they duly became the SA1, 2 and 3 classes. The Ministry had given the Board permission to operate the wider vehicles in the outer area of the capital only, and Ilford depot was chosen as their base. Deliveries started in November 1941 and were complete by April 1943.

In May 1941 a notice was issued to announce that services would be withdrawn an hour earlier than usual during the summer months, one of many austerity measures taken at this time.

The trolleybuses diverted from South Africa due to shipping restrictions, were a welcome addition to the fleet between November 1941 and April 1943. They relieved the pressure on the Board and enabled them to return the borrowed Bournemouth trolleybuses. SA2 class No.1746 looks splendid in this view on the 693 at Chadwell Heath. It was delivered in July 1942. The route number plate was needed as the smaller side blind could not satisfactorily accommodate the route number. *W. J. Haynes*

When the new schedules were announced in October 1942, it was decided that the trolleybus operations should follow the path already being used by Central Buses. Vehicles from outer London depots would be parked up at inner London depots during non-peak hours, to avoid lost mileage and save on vital energy supplies. Although the hectic days of the Blitz were now past, there were still occasional encounters with the enemy. One particularly unsavoury incident took place in Ilford High Road on March 12th 1943, when the area was bombed and machine gunned. An Inspector on a trolleybus was shot and killed during this raid.

The worst incident regarding loss of vehicles during the war was at Bexleyheath on 29th June 1944. Flying bombs were now the biggest threat to Londoners, and when the depot was struck by one of these its operations were paralysed. Twenty-six trolleybuses had their bodies destroyed: 390, 391, 392, 395, 405, 407, 409, 451, 766, 784, 786, 790, 794, 799, 801, 804 and 808, which were later rebodied by East Lancs, and 97, 98, 385, 389, 396, 397, 402, 415 and 419, which received new bodies from Northern Coachbuilders. Twelve trolleybuses were completely destroyed, 99, 386, 387, 394, 398, 418, 428, 435, 448, 787, 791 and 812. All other vehicles in the depot were also in need of attention the following day and, although other trolleybuses were brought in from around the network, motor buses were drafted in to help provide a service.

Not all damage to the fleet was inflicted by the enemy. On 19th June 1942, N1 class No.1581 somehow managed to overturn at Ilford whilst on route 663. Quite what happened we shall never know, but the recovery crews are well on their way to restoring the vehicle to an upright position. Its booms have been removed before the process begins. *Mirrorpix*

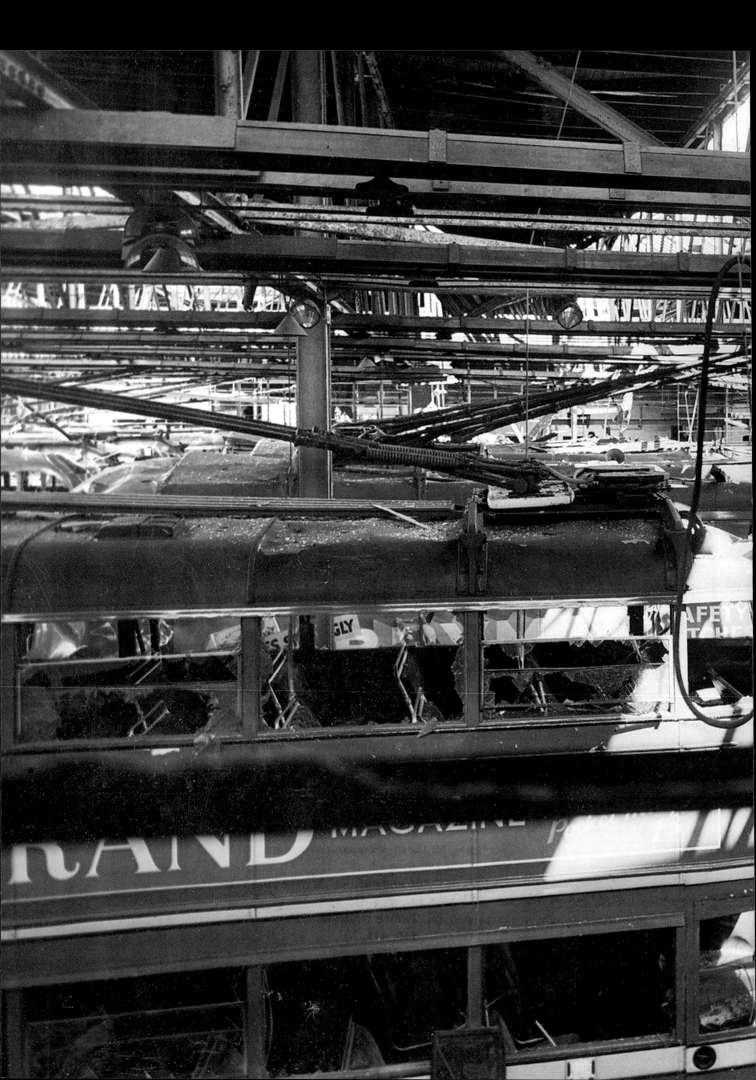

In July 1944, T.E. Thomas, General Manager of Trams and Trolleybuses, received a letter from A.C. Baker, the General Manager of Birmingham City Transport, offering to lend the Board some trolleybuses. Thomas agreed to send someone to look at the vehicles "to see if we could put them into a usable state". An inspection was duly carried out, but the offer was politely declined.

By far the most tragic occurrence involving a trolleybus took place in Dames Road, near Wanstead Flats, on 27th July 1944. West Ham's class L3 No.1387 had a full load when it was completely destroyed by a flying bomb which exploded between it and some houses. Only three days later, on the 30th, West Ham depot

Overleaf Carnage at Bexleyheath depot on 29th June 1944. A flying bomb struck in the early hours and the building suffered tremendous damage. Twelve trolleybuses were completely destroyed, and twenty-six had their bodies damaged beyond repair. This was the second time the depot had been hit, a previous raid on 7th November 1940 destroying the bodies of four vehicles. *LT Museum*

Another flying bomb attack caused extensive damage to the Falk Stadelman building near Hatton Garden on 24th August 1944. K1 1138 was caught up in the blast, and receives some attention to its trolley booms. *Mirrorpix*

and works were hit again. This time it was far worse than the 1941 episode. Eighteen trolleybuses had their bodies destroyed and one, 364, was written off completely. Later rebodied by East Lancs were: 412, 470, 993, 1001A, 1007, 1385, 1543 and 1545. Northern Coachbuilders supplied the new bodies for: 430, 578, 602, 623, 626, 629, 633, 635, 641 and 643. The interesting vehicle here is 1385. Being a chassisless L3, there was not a basis for rebodying, but the chassis of 364 was salvaged, fitted with newer electrical equipment and the new East Lancs body; it was re-classified N1B. The last serious incident to involve the fleet happened on 16th August 1944. E1 class 575 was working from Walthamstow on the 697 when it was caught at the junction of Hoe Street and High Street. The body was destroyed and the driver and some passengers were killed. The vehicle received a new Northern Coachbuilders body in May 1946. In addition to the rebodied vehicles, and the extensive work carried out at Charlton, West Ham and Fulwell works, J.C.Beadle of Dartford also rebuilt eight trolleybuses in 1944 and 1945. Two of these, 406A and 1123A, were rebuilt after blast damage at West Ham in the July 1944 episode, and the others, 393, 400, 403, 416, 807 and 811, after damage in the June 1944 Bexleyheath incident. It should be noted that of the rebodied trolleybuses, four were short-wheelbase 60-seat B1 class vehicles; 95, 97, 98 and 107. When supplied with new bodies, these chassis were rebuilt to the standard length and re-classified D2C.

As the war came to a close, sixty-one trolleybuses had had their bodies written off. Sixteen were rebodied by Weymann during the war years, a further twenty-five would be dealt with by East Lancs between 1945 and 1948, and the other twenty by Northern Coachbuilders between December 1945 and September 1946. In addition to these, seventeen trolleybuses were completely destroyed.

The V2 rocket was a devastating successor to the V1 flying bomb. One hit Ilford with disastrous results on 8th February 1945. Two tower wagons with crews are at work to restore some sense of order, but it will be a while before the Civil Defence and fire crews can clear the road. Between 1940 and 1945, temporary wires had to be erected in many places and on many occasions so that trolleybuses could by-pass craters or other bomb damage. *Mirrorpix*

This chapter looks at each trolleybus depot, the routes operated and the main changes to those routes during their lifetimes. The depots are shown in alphabetical order of their original names and some were renamed in 1950. All vehicle requirements shown for January 1959 are after the schedule revisions of the 7th of that month.

ACTON

The former London United Tramways depot in the High Street at Acton was never part of the London Transport plan for trolleybus operation. The site did feature however, as a temporary measure, housing trolleybuses when conversion work was still being undertaken at other depots. C2, C3 and D2 class vehicles were used. This period of operation was confined to 1936 and 1937, and can be summarised as follows:

Route 607. Commenced 15th November 1936. Acton operated a few trolleybuses between 13th December 1936 and 9th March 1937.

Route 655. Commenced 13th December 1936, operated jointly with Hanwell until 9th March 1937 (Mon-Sat).

Route 660. Operated between Acton Market Place and Hammersmith only when introduced on 5th April 1936, and worked by Acton from the outset. Operated again together with Finchley and Stonebridge depots from North Finchley to Hammersmith from 8th February 1937 until 9th March 1937.

Route 666. Edgware to Hammersmith daily, worked from 5th July 1936 until 12th December 1936 with Hendon and from 23rd August 1936 until 13th December with Stonebridge.

Operations ceased 9th March 1937.

The depot was never operational again with London Transport, although the electrical engineers department made use of the building for some time. Its last use was by CentreWest Buses, as a garage and workshops between 27th March 1993 and 15th March 2008. It has since been demolished.

Acton depot was a typical Victorian building, and London United began electric tram services from here in 1901. It was never intended to operate trolleybuses, and the period of use was limited to 1936 and 1937. D2 461 pokes its front out into the daylight, blinded up for the 655.
LT Museum

Maximum vehicles used:
February 1937

607	11
655	11
660ex	4

BEXLEYHEATH

The area served by this depot was completely isolated from the rest of the system. Had the tram to trolleybus conversion scheme not been curtailed because of the Second World War, this would not have been the case; the tram routes south of the river operated by New Cross and Abbey Wood would have been converted to trolleybuses, and the connection at Woolwich to the Bexleyheath routes would have been made. Bexleyheath was the only completely new depot to have been constructed for trolleybuses by London Transport, the Erith and Bexleyheath Corporation depots having been deemed as unsuitable. The new depot had a capacity of 75 vehicles and was provided with a wired circuit around the perimeter of the building for testing and training purposes. Separate sheds were also built for a tower wagon and breakdown lorry.

When the Bexley area routes were converted in 1935, the Board had inspected the Bexley and Erith Council depots, and had decided that neither were suited for the purpose of operating the new trolleybuses. For the first and only time during the conversion scheme, a completely new depot was built on a new site in Erith Road. It was light and spacious, and had a large forecourt and yard at the rear. *LT Museum*

Operations at Bexleyheath were a mere three days away when this view of B2 class 113 was taken on 7th November 1935. It shows the tiled pit area in the new depot, a far superior working environment to the one in which the maintenance staff were used to in tram days. *LT Museum*

The area of operation varied widely in type from densely populated and industrial to the new semi-detached, and countrified, areas of North Kent. Tram route 98 was replaced on 10th November 1935, with new trolleybus route 698 following exactly the tram routeing between Woolwich and Bexleyheath, via Abbey Wood and Erith. On 24th November enough new vehicles were available to allow trams on the 96 to be replaced by route 696. This operated between Woolwich and Dartford, via Welling and Crayford, but was not projected to Horns Cross (the terminus in tram days), this section being covered by country bus route 480. New short wheelbase 60-seat class B2s were used, but as the area expanded with new housing, and with workers at the Woolwich Arsenal and surrounding factories, they were soon to prove inadequate. Photographic evidence exists of Diddlers operating from the depot, but it is not clear whether these were as trainers or as stop-gap service buses. Newer 70 seat vehicles from the D2 and H1 classes, and C1s borrowed from Fulwell and new B1s were drafted in to provide the extra capacity needed. During the mid-forties, D2s and H1s provided the mainstay of the fleet, although many other classes featured whilst the war damaged vehicles were under repair. A third route, numbered 694, working from Woolwich to Erith via Bexleyheath was introduced on 16th May 1937 to run pm only on Sundays and Bank Holidays. This working ceased on 28th January 1940 and, although reinstated during the summer periods of the war years, it last appeared on 22nd October 1944. Route 696 was always the more heavily used and more frequent route, and served the busy shopping areas in Welling and

You can almost feel the cold as H1 class 805 creeps along through the snow on route 696. No one is about in this early 1950s scene, and the driver will have to be very cautious when he negotiates West Hill in Dartford. *Mick Webber Collection*

Bexleyheath on its way into the Kent towns of Crayford and Dartford. The 698, its quieter and less frequent partner, shared the same route as the 696 as far as Plumstead Corner, where the two parted company. The 698 then shared the tram wires to Abbey Wood, and then on through the relatively quiet Lower Belvedere into Erith, and through the expanding semi-detached Barnehurst to Bexleyheath, where the two routes converged. The cramped terminus at the Woolwich Free Ferry was superseded on 14th July 1943 by a new and more spacious one at Parsons Hill. Bexleyheath trolleybuses were towed to Charlton works when extensive repairs or overhauls were to be carried out. As mentioned earlier, the depot was hit twice during the war, the occasions being on 7th November 1940 and 29th June 1944.

When the decision to abandon the trolleybus system in favour of motorbuses was taken, the Bexleyheath routes were earmarked to be included in the first stage. This duly took place, the last day of operation being 3rd March 1959, RT family buses being used in replacement. The building still serves as a bus garage for TfL contracted services.

Maximum vehicles operated
October 1938: **696 – 40. 698 – 18.**
March 1946:   **696 – 59. 698 – 21** (Sat pm).
May 1950:   **696 – 59. 698 – 22.**
January 1959: **696 – 51. 698 – 14**

A short working turn was provided at Walnut Tree Road for route 698, and H1B 799B stands in the layby provided. The Burndept warehouse is the backdrop, and behind that is the River Thames. The date is 31st August 1958. *N.Rayfield 2RT2 Group*

45

BOW

Bow was previously an LCC tram depot and was opened in June 1908 to serve the busy Bow Road routes. When converted for trolleybuses, it had a capacity of 102. Situated in Fairfield Road, it was just off line of the main Bow Road and had one traverser and a turntable. The new trolleybuses began service on 5th November 1939 on routes 661 from Leyton to Aldgate and the 663 between Ilford and Aldgate. The two shared the same roads from Aldgate through Stepney, Bow and Stratford, and there they diverged; the 661 to Leytonstone High Road and Whipps Cross to Leyton depot, and the 663 along the Romford Road to Ilford. At the Leyton terminus, 661 buses turned on the loop through Leyton depot and stood on the forecourt.

New trolleybuses of the M1, N1 and N2 classes provided the service. Bow always had the N classes throughout its existence as a trolleybus depot. On 29th October 1941 another new route, the 695, was introduced to run from Bow Church to Chadwell Heath on Mondays to Saturdays, duplicating the 663 as far as Ilford, then running on to Seven Kings and Chadwell Heath. This was the last new London trolleybus route, and its operation was shared with Ilford from 10th November 1948. The section between Stratford and Aldgate was exceptionally busy, despite the parallel bus services, and the service intervals quoted in the early fifties were every 3 to 4 minutes for the 661 and every 2 to 4 minutes for the 663 on Monday to Fridays.

The London County Council Tramways department built the depot in Fairfield Road Bow in 1908. London Transport converted it to trolleybus operation in November 1939, a couple of months into the hostilities. Its working of electric traction continued for another 20 years before finally surrendering to the motor bus in 1959.
LT Museum

It is 18th July 1959 and exactly one month later Bow will cease to be a trolleybus depot. N1 1621 enters the building. *John Gillham*

Passenger numbers suffered badly in the mid-fifties, when the railway line from Liverpool Street was electrified. The 695 was withdrawn on 6th January 1959 just before the main conversion scheme came into being, the 663 being extended to Chadwell Heath to compensate. Despite the N class vehicles being among the newest in the fleet, Bow depot was converted to RTL buses in stage three of the scheme after services on 18th August 1959, its trolleybuses being moved on to replace older trolleybuses elsewhere. The building survives and continues in use as a bus garage.

Maximum vehicles operated:
April 1941:   **661** – 43. **663** – 45.
March 1946:   **661** – 46. **663** – 48. **695** – 13.
May 1950:   **661** – 35. **663** – 52. **695** – 22.
January 1959: **661** – 27. **663** – 36.

CHISWICK

It was never intended to use the former LUT tram depot at Chiswick for trolleybuses, but the work being carried out at Hammersmith to accommodate the new vehicles was causing a temporary lack of space. Some D2 and D3 class trolleybuses on routes 626, 628 and 630 were worked from here from September 1937 while officially allocated to Hammersmith depot. They worked dead to and from the Broadway, the crews signing on and cashing in at Hammersmith.

This arrangement ceased around the end of 1937, and the only evidence found of the operations is in traffic circulars. One from September 1937 states that vehicles working from Chiswick depot on the 626/628 should not carry passengers between the depot and Hammersmith Broadway in either direction, and that Private must be shown. A further circular from the same month instructs conductors that the frog at King Street Junction should be pulled for Chiswick, and also that at Chiswick Depot the trolleys should be changed on to the running-in wires when entering and leaving the depot.

10	15½	CHELVERTON ROAD	
8	21½	3½	CHISWICK TROLLEYBUS DEPOT
9	22½	4½	1½	CHISWICK WORKS

No photographs of Chiswick depot operating trolleybuses appear to exist, but this section of a mileage chart compiled by the Board does, however, show that it was given that title.

EDMONTON

Edmonton was a former Metropolitan Electric Tramways depot built in 1880, situated appropriately in Tramway Avenue. It was extensively rebuilt by London Transport for trolleybus operation with a total capacity of 122, and had one traverser and turntable until late in 1950, when the traverser and turntable from Wandsworth were moved here and installed in the same pit. Accommodation was also provided for a tower wagon and breakdown lorry, with access from Causey Ware Road. Trolleybus operation commenced on 16th October 1938 using new members of the K class. On this date tram routes 59 and 79 were withdrawn, along with part of the 49, and replaced by new routes 659 working from Waltham Cross to Holborn and route 679 from Smithfield to Ponders End (extended to Waltham Cross on Sundays). The northern section of the 49 was replaced by route 649, running between Stamford Hill and Ponders End. At this time, Holloway alone operated route 679, with Edmonton taking an allocation on 14th December, when the route was extended to Waltham Cross Mon-Fri peaks and Sats. It assumed full responsibility on 5th February 1939, when the route worked to Waltham Cross at all times. Tram route 27 was replaced on 6th November 1938 by new route 627, which ran between Edmonton Town Hall and Tottenham Court Road. Edmonton ran this route alone until 5th February 1939, when Holloway and Wood Green were given allocations. The southern section of tram route 49 was withdrawn on 5th February 1939 and the 649 extended to Liverpool Street. The 649, 659 and 679 provided an intense service along the Hertford Road, being joined by the 627, and they shared the wires until the junction with Seven Sisters Road. At this point the 649 continued south through Stamford Hill, Stoke Newington and Dalston to its destination at Liverpool Street. The other routes continued down Seven Sisters Road to the junctions at Manor House and Nags Head, where they split up. The 627 continued down Camden Road to Camden

The Metropolitan Electric Tramways had built their depot at Edmonton in 1880. When London Transport converted it to trolleybuses in 1938 it was completely rebuilt. After conversion to buses in 1961 it continued in use until 1986. *N.Rayfield 2RT2 Group*

Edmonton was a deceptively large depot, and operated mainly K and P1 class Leyland trolleybuses. K class 1233, 1231 and 1344 can be seen in this view. *John Gillham*

Town, past Mornington Crescent, and on to the new terminal loop at Tottenham Court Road. Going back to the Nags Head, the 659 turned left and then into Caledonian Road, turning at the Holborn loop in a clockwise direction. The 679 also turned left at the Nags Head, but traversed Holloway Road and Upper Street, Islington down to Smithfield. On 14th May 1939 the 649 was extended to Waltham Cross on Sundays, and on 5th May 1948 the arrangement was made daily.

Edmonton routes worked through a densely populated part of London, and the first allocation of new trolleybuses to the depot were the all-Leyland K class vehicles, some of which remained there all of their lives. Waltham Cross had the distinction of being the most northerly terminus on the London trolleybus system, and these routes also played a large part in moving the crowds after Tottenham Hotspur home matches at White Hart Lane, the bulk of the routes in this section being trolleybus rather than bus. Over 30 extras were run on these occasions, with trolleybuses being loaned to Edmonton by Wood Green and Stamford Hill depots among others. The service along the Hertford Road was one of the most intense on the London system. The later batch of Leylands delivered in 1940, the K3s, were all allocated to Edmonton and spent nearly all of their time there. In post-war years, the P1 class also had a large representation at the depot along with some H1s.

Major withdrawal of trolleybuses from the depot was part of stage ten on 25th April 1961, when routes 627, 659 and 679 ceased to operate. The remaining 649 lingered on alongside the new Routemasters until stage eleven on 18th July, when it too was withdrawn, and Edmonton ceased to operate electric traction. The building continued as a bus garage until 1st February 1986, when it closed. It was demolished for new housing.

Maximum vehicles operated:
October 1938: **649** – 21. **659** – 40. **627** – 33 (Nov) **679** – 2 (Dec).
March 1946:   **627** – 10. **649** – 38. **659** – 56. **679** – 25.
May 1950:   **627** – 10. **649** – 42. **659** – 49. **679** – 25.
January 1959: **627** – 12. **649** – 39. **659** – 32. **679** – 27.

FINCHLEY

The Metropolitan Electric Tramways shed at Finchley was in Woodberry Grove and opened in 1905. It operated trams and trolleybuses alongside each other at the beginning of the conversion programme in 1936. The capacity of the depot for trolleybuses was 108, and it had a turntable and traverser. Sheds were also provided for a tower wagon and breakdown lorry. Vehicles of the C classes together with the J1 and J2 were the first to be operated. This remained until the final years, when some L3, M1 and N2 class were drafted in. The first trolleybuses appeared on 2nd August 1936 when routes 645 and 660 were introduced. The 645 was worked together with Hendon and ran from Edgware to North Finchley via Cricklewood and Golders Green. The 660 had originally started on 5th April 1936 in a shorter form and was withdrawn just three months later on 4th July. The new 660 operated from North Finchley to Hammersmith via Golders Green, Cricklewood, Harlesden and Acton. It was shared with Acton and, from 23rd August, with Stonebridge. Also, by 5th July, Finchley was additionally operating route 666 (Mons-Sats).

The next influx of trolleybuses to the depot was on 6th March 1938, when routes 521, 621 and 651 began operations. The 521 and 621 worked from North Finchley to the Holborn loop via New Southgate, Wood Green, Manor House, Nags Head and Kings Cross. The former tram termini at Holborn had been at Farringdon Road and Grays Inn Road, but now these two points were joined by wiring up Charterhouse Street and Holborn to form a loop. This loop worked thus: 600 series numbers worked the clockwise direction and the 500 series anti-clockwise. The 651 has the dubious record for being the shortest-lived London trolleybus route. It ran from Barnet to Golders Green on Mon-Fri peaks, and Sat and Sun pm, being extended to Cricklewood Mon-Fri off peaks. The route was withdrawn on 31st May 1938. Routes 617 and 517 had been introduced on 6th and 7th March 1938 respectively, running from North Finchley to the Holborn loop via Highgate and the Nags Head, then via the 521/621, and were operated by Holloway. These routes were switched to Finchley on 1st June, where they remained until reverting to Holloway on 29th October 1941. Starting on 8th January 1939, route 617 was discontinued on Sundays, being replaced by route

The MET depot at Finchley was in Woodberry Grove and this view shows the scene in December 1936. It remained largely untouched when converted to trolleybuses. Its tower wagon can be seen parked in front of the shed that was provided. *LT Museum*

517. The 645 was extended at both ends on 1st June 1938, from Edgware to Canons Park, and from North Finchley to Barnet. Route 609 commenced 6th March 1938 between Barnet and Moorgate, being worked by Holloway, although Finchley worked the route on Sundays pm between Barnet and Islington Green from 14th May 1939. The route was transferred to Finchley on 29th October 1941, and remained their sole responsibility until 9th November 1952, when Highgate took a share of the Sunday workings.

   The first routes to be lost in the trolleybus-to-bus scheme were at stage twelve on 7th November 1961, when the 521/621 and 609 bowed out, the remaining routes 645 and 660 finishing on 2nd January 1962 in stage thirteen. It remained as a bus garage until 4th December 1993, when it was closed and later demolished.

Maximum vehicles operated:

October 1938:	**521/621** – 40.	**517/617** – 31.	**645/660/666** – 26.
March 1946:	**521/621** – 32.	**609** – 31.	**645/660/666** – 18.
May 1950:	**521/621** – 32.	**609** – 31.	**645/660** – 21.
January 1959:	**521/621** – 29.	**609** – 26.	**645** – 9. **660** – 8.

This interior view of Finchley, also in December 1936, shows the traverser and pit. Trolleybus 323 is the vehicle on the right. Note that vehicles during this early period, had advertising each side of the rear destination display. *LT Museum*

FULWELL

Fulwell is the spiritual home of the London trolleybus. A large imposing depot, it was opened by the London United Tramways in April 1903 with access from both Stanley Road and Wellington Road. A large overhaul works with a traverser also existed as part of the building, and a shed for a tower wagon was provided. The capacity was 120 vehicles. London United Tramways decided that this form of transport was the way forward, and a fleet of new AEC trolleybuses with UCC bodywork, and nicknamed 'Diddlers', transformed the routes in this part of south west London. The beginning was on 16th May 1931, when a service numbered 1 began between Twickenham and Teddington. As the new wiring progressed, it was soon extended into Kingston and around a loop via Park Road, Kings Road and Richmond Road, the loop being worked in both directions. On 15th July, route 1 was diverted at Kingston to run through Surbiton and on to a turn at Tolworth Red Lion, and new route 2 worked from Tolworth via the same route into Kingston and then via the loop in both directions. Route 2 changed again on 29th July. Now it ran from Tolworth into Kingston, around the loop in an anti-clockwise direction, back to Surbiton and on to the Dittons. New route 3 traversed the same roads, but worked the loop in a clockwise direction.

On 2nd September 1931, new route 4 replaced trams on the Hampton Court to Wimbledon route, passing through Kingston, Malden and Raynes Park, and in 1932 (the date is unknown) route 5 started between Teddington and Malden as a Saturday pm working. It later became a daily route on 8th May 1940, by now numbered 605, working Mon–Fri peak hours to Wimbledon and to Malden at other times. Many changes were made to the route over the years, and the final one was on 11th January 1959, when it was extended on Sundays to Twickenham.

On 20th September 1933, by now under the control of the LPTB, a previously authorised extension to the trolleybus service from the Red Lion at Tolworth to work an anti-clockwise loop at Tolworth Bypass came into use. Routes 1 and 3 were both extended to the bypass, but overprovision soon became obvious and route 3 was cut back within a year to its original stand at the Red Lion. On the

The former London United depot at Fulwell was where it all began. The LUT had the foresight to invest in the trolleybus, and the legacy was continued by London Transport. This late view showing two L3 class vehicles, No 1489 and 1444, clearly shows the enamel tram road numbers above the doors and covered-over tram tracks. *Mike Beamish*

The Q1 class is nearing its end at Fulwell depot, and they will be heading abroad to end their days. 1811 is on the 603 in Kingston heading for the Richmond Park loop on 15th January 1961, where it will travel in a clockwise direction, before heading back to Tolworth. *Norman Rayfield/2RT2 Group*

same date, the Kingston loop routes were revised to work as follows: route 2 The Dittons to Kingston Loop working anti-clockwise, and route 3, Tolworth Red Lion to Kingston Loop working clockwise. One short-lived route was the 1A, which operated from Tolworth Red Lion to Surbition in morning peaks. After London Transport took control, the routes were renumbered in the summer of 1935 to 601-605. The initially infrequent 5 and then 605 became a daily route from 8th May 1940. The 1A was renumbered 601A, but this never appeared on the blinds and the route was withdrawn in 1943. After deciding to continue where the LUT left off, the Board were committed to replacing the rest of the ageing tram fleet with trolleybuses. The obvious next step was to finish off the conversion of operations at Fulwell, replacing the remaining trams there and at nearby Hounslow. New route 667 began on 27th October 1935 from Hammersmith to Chiswick, Kew, Brentford, Busch Corner, Twickenham and Hampton Court. This was the first time the newly designed London Transport standard trolleybuses were used.

This view is taken from the Stanley Road entrance at Fulwell. Tram lines are still in evidence with the cobblestones and L3 1395 is parked centre stage. A group of withdrawn trolleybuses are parked on the left waiting their fate. It is Sunday 8th April 1962, and there is but one month of operation left. *John Laker*

Bank Holiday special workings took place on this route, with a mixture of extras from Hammersmith and Shepherds Bush to Hampton Court, vehicles showing 667 when working to Hammersmith, and 657 when working to Shepherds Bush. These extras were also worked by Hounslow and Hanwell depots. After the war, the new Q1 class 8ft-wide trolleybuses were operated from Fulwell and Hounslow and, after service reductions, from Hanwell.

The Fulwell routes were to form stage fourteen of the conversion scheme, the final chapter in the London trolleybus story. By this time, older L3 class buses were working the six routes, and they all ceased on 8th May 1962, bringing to an end nearly 31 years of trolleybus operation. L3 class No.1521 arrived on the 604 in the early hours of 9th May amidst a large crowd that assembled to celebrate the occasion. The premises are still operational as a bus garage.

Fulwell was provided with many rooflights, and therefore had a lot of natural light, as can be seen here. Through working was possible due to the gates at either end in Stanley Road and Wellington Road. L3 class 1526 is featured here nearing the end of trolleybus operation.
Mike Beamish

Maximum vehicles operated:
October 1938: **601/2/3** – 34. **604** – 20. **605** – 8. **667** – 21.
March 1946: **601/602/603** – 34. **604** – 26. **605** – 10. **667** – 26.
May 1950: **601/2/3** – 34. **604** – 27. **605** – 16. **667** – 30.
January 1959: **601** – 19. **602** – 4. **603** – 5. **604/5** – 21. **667** – 23.

HACKNEY (Clapton)

The LCC depot at Bohemia Place, Hackney was opened in March 1909 and was converted for trolleybus operation on 11th June 1939. The depot had a capacity of 90 vehicles, and was provided with a traverser and turntable. The first trolley-buses to be allocated here were a mixture of new and secondhand Leyland K1 and K2s, which commenced new route 581 between Bloomsbury and Woodford via Rosebery Avenue, Dalston, Hackney and Leyton. K1s and K2s remained the types operated throughout the depot's life. The operation was shared with Walthamstow, although that depot's share was replaced by Leyton on 8th May 1940. Also on 11th June route 555 started, which ran from Bloomsbury to Leyton, Downsell Road (Leyton Green on Sundays). This was initially operated by Leyton, with the odd journey worked by Hackney, but on 10th December 1939 this alloca-tion was increased to 10. The route was extended on Sunday to Woodford from 12th May 1940 until November 1948 and then the extension was resumed on 11th October 1953, running on Sunday afternoons. The 555 travelled via Clerkenwell Road, Old Street, Cambridge Heath Road and Hackney, where it met the 581 and shared the wires as far as the Baker's Arms, where it headed north to Woodford. Hackney received a third route on 10th September 1939, just a week after the declaration of war; this was the 677, for which it assumed full control. The route worked in an inverted U shape from Smithfield, through the Angel, Dalston, Hackney, Victoria Park, Mile End and across East India Dock Road to West India Docks. This was a very busy route, catering for market workers at one end and dockers at the other and, in good weather, visitors to Victoria Park. With these route introductions, the tram in London no longer held the majority in electric road traction.

The depot was an early casualty in the replacement scheme, all routes being replaced in stage two by RTL buses after service on 14th April 1959. Bus operation continues from this site.

Maximum vehicles operated:

April 1941:	**555** – 36.	**581** – 7.	**677** – 33.
March 1946:	**555** – 36.	**581** – 12.	**677** – 27.
May 1950:	**555** – 37.	**581** – 8.	**677** – 29.
January 1959:	**555** – 22.	**581** – 11.	**677** – 25.

Hackney depot, later to be renamed Clapton, was associated with the K1 and 2 class Leylands throughout its life as a trolleybus depot. One of them, K1 No.1300, is shown here in this late view in 1959. The builder's board is displayed prominently, as work is under way for the conversion. *N. Rayfield, 2RT2 Group*

HAMMERSMITH

Hammersmith was a former LCC tram shed standing in Great Church Lane and opened in 1908, a very busy year for depot building. The rebuilding was substantial, and the area at the front which had previously been in the open, was now covered and formed part of the new and larger depot. It had a traverser and turntable and a capacity for 65 trolleybuses. 12th September 1937 saw the introduction of the new vehicles when routes 628 and 630 commenced, with the 626 starting the next day. D2 and D3 class vehicles were used here, the D2s being secondhand from Hanwell. Hammersmith also worked some P1s alongside a small allocation of F1s. The 628 worked from Clapham Junction to Craven Park on Mon-Sats and Harrow Road on Sundays, running via Wandsworth, Putney, Fulham, Hammersmith, Shepherds Bush and Harlesden. It was extended to Wembley Mon-Fri evenings for the greyhound racing between 4th August 1938 and 21st November 1939, and from this date the Mon-Sat evening journeys worked as far as Scrubs Lane only. On 19th October 1949, the route became daily from Craven Park to Clapham Junction. The 628 also had a night service between Hammersmith and Clapham Junction, which ran unnumbered until 19th June 1946. This continued until October 1950, when the route was revised to run to Tooting, and then numbered 630. Route 630 operated from West Croydon to Harrow Road, Scrubs Lane and served Mitcham, Tooting, Wandsworth, Putney, Hammersmith and Shepherds Bush. The stand at Scrubs Lane was in Letchford Gardens, being wired in an anti-clockwise loop via Waldo Road, Letchford Gardens, Harrow Road, and Scrubs Lane. On 15th January 1940, an extension off line of route came into use, when wiring along Wimbledon Road and Plough Lane, was used to serve Wimbledon Stadium Greyhound track.

Hammersmith contributed to peak hours work on the Harlesden to Acton (later extended to Hammersmith Broadway) section over the years, starting on 22nd November 1939. Initially numbered 666, these weekday peak extras became 660s from 20th October 1943. This operation continued until 30th September 1950, when they were transferred to Stonebridge.

The 626 was a Mon-Sat peak hour service from Acton Market Place to Clapham Junction, working to Harlesden and then following the 628 to Shepherds Bush, and sharing the wires all the way to Clapham Junction. These routes were heavily involved in the extra crowds for the boat race, Fulham Football Club and White City greyhound racing. Mitcham Fair also required extra workings, and these were supplied by Sutton. The 626 and 628 had some workings from Stonebridge and the 630 from Wandsworth. The end for Hammersmith came at stage seven on 19th July 1960 and, as the depot was to close to traffic, replacing buses worked from Shepherds Bush garage. After closure, the depot became the home of the BEA coaches that London Transport operated on behalf of the airline. The coaches were moved to Chiswick tram depot in 1966 and the depot at Hammersmith was closed. The site has since been re-developed.

Maximum vehicles used:
October 1938: **626/628** – 22. **630** – 32.
March 1946: **626/628** – 22. **630** – 42. **660** – 6.
May 1950: **626/628** – 22. **630** – 48. **660** – 4.
January 1959: **626/628** – 16. **630** – 45.

HANWELL

The former London United Tramways depot in Hanwell Broadway was built in 1901 and was operating the new Feltham cars on trunk route 7 when London Transport started to prepare the shed for the new trolleybuses. It was completely rebuilt and the Feltham trams were eventually moved out to be prepared for their trip to south London, where they would be also using the conduit method of current collection. A turntable and traverser were installed in the depot, which had a capacity of 108 vehicles and separate sheds for a tower wagon and breakdown lorry. New D2 class trolleybuses were the first inhabitants. The new 607, beginning on 15th November 1936, worked from Shepherds Bush via Acton, Ealing, Hanwell, Southall and Hayes to Uxbridge, where it was extended about half a mile beyond the tram terminus to a new turning point just east of the junction with Harefield Road. More trolleybuses operated on this route than any other on the London system. From March 1937, the D2s were gradually replaced by new F1 class trolleybuses, which had more powerful motors and were better suited to the long run along the Uxbridge Road. Some H1, K1 and K2 trolleybuses also worked from here. As building work was still progressing at the depot, Acton helped with the operations between December 1936 and March 1937. Hanwell also operated Bank Holiday extras from Shepherds Bush to Hampton Court.

Hanwell's other route, the 655, commenced on 13th December 1936 and worked Mon-Sat from Hammersmith to Acton Market Place via Chiswick, Brentford and Hanwell, being extended on Mon-Sat peak hours to Craven Park. On Sundays it ran from Hammersmith to Hanwell but, as no turn was yet available at the depot, it ran on to a turn at Hanwell Hospital Gates, which was a circle opposite Hanwell (later Southall) bus garage. When the new side entrance to Hanwell depot had been constructed onto Jessamine Road, trolleybuses on the 655 used this as its turning point from 14th March 1937. The route was also worked in part by Acton until 9th March 1937. The 655 had many alterations over the years, and the main changes can be summarised as follows. From 10th March 1937 the Craven Park section was withdrawn, as was the section from Acton to Hanwell in Mon-Sat

The former London United depot at Hanwell was demolished and replaced by this modern new trolleybus depot. The staff were provided with a comfortable and light office and administration building, and the depot was given a new side entrance with access from Jessamine Road. This view shows the frontage in May 1937 just seven months into trolleybus operation.
LT Museum

off-peaks. Hanwell worked extras on route 666 on weekdays, which it inherited from Acton on 10th March 1937. These worked between Acton, Horn Lane and Hammersmith, until withdrawn in September the same year. At the same time, it took on 666 extras between Craven Park and Acton, Horn Lane on weekday peak hours. These were transferred to route 660 from 19th May 1943. The Saturday workings survived until November 1947, and the Mon-Fri work until April 1949.

A major extension of the 655 took place on 12th September 1937 when it was projected to Clapham Junction daily, now running Acton to Clapham Junction Mon-Sat peaks and Hanwell to Clapham Junction the rest of the time. The Clapham Junction journeys on weekday evenings and Sundays were cut back to Hammersmith Broadway from 22nd November 1939. On 5th April 1942, the Sunday service was cut back to run from Hanwell to Brentford only. From 21st April 1943, the Clapham Junction leg ran during peak hours only, and from 16th June 1946 the Sunday service ran between Hanwell and Hammersmith from 10am until 9pm. Between October 1956 and October 1959, the route worked in two sections: Acton Vale to Brentford, and Hanwell to Clapham Junction. On 10th January 1959, the route was Acton Vale to Clapham Junction Mon-Fri peaks and Hanwell to Hammersmith the rest of the time.

In January 1953, the depot received its first trolleybuses of the Q1 class. These were from the second batch built in 1952 and worked on the 607. Hanwell was involved in stage eight of the trolleybus conversion scheme on 8th November 1960 and remained a bus garage until 27th March 1993, when it was closed. It has since been demolished.

Maximum vehicles used:
October 1938: **607** – 59. **655** – 25
March 1946:   **607** – 74. **655** – 31. **660** – 2.
May 1950:   **607** – 80. **655** – 34.
January 1959: **607** – 66. **655** – 26.

The mainstay of the Hanwell fleet were the F1 class Leylands. Two of these, numbers 707 and 716, are seen here blinded and ready for the 655. The depot could boast that it operated the most trolleybuses on any one route in London, which at one stage was eighty on the 607. *John Gillham*

HENDON (Colindale)

The depot here was in Edgware Road, and was previously owned by the Metropolitan Electric Tramways, who opened it in 1904. An overhaul works also existed here where London United and South Met trams were dealt with, as well as the MET's own fleet. A very early experimental trolleybus was tried here in 1909, although nothing further materialised.

When converted for trolleybuses, a turning area was constructed at the rear and a shed for a breakdown vehicle was provided, though for most of its life it was bricked up and Hendon/Colindale called on other depots to attend disabled trolleybuses. A large area behind the depot was used to scrap the withdrawn trams. The capacity was for 48 trolleybuses, the first of which were AEC C types. After the Bow conversion in 1959, Colindale received N1 class AECs which they kept until the end. Hendon's first trolleybus route was the 666 which was introduced on 5th July 1936, running from Edgware to Hammersmith and serving Cricklewood, Willesden, Harlesden and Acton. This route was operated by Hendon and Acton on introduction. On 23rd August 1936 it became a weekday peaks and Sun pm route only. It continued in this form until 5th May 1940, when the Sunday workings were withdrawn. They were reinstated on 23rd April 1944 and withdrawn again on 22nd October 1944. The Sunday workings were introduced yet again on 6th May 1945 and then, on 4th June 1949, the Saturday workings were lost, followed by the Sunday work on 16th October 1949, leaving the route as a Mon-Fri peak only operation from this date.

Hendon depot was inherited from the MET and completely rebuilt for the new trolleybuses. A turning area was built at the rear, and therefore a traverser was not needed. The new office block has yet to be completed on the right in this view taken from the Edgware Road early in 1936. *LT Museum*

The next new route affecting Hendon came on 2nd August 1936, when the 645 appeared in an operation shared with Finchley depot, where its route is detailed. The last arrival at Hendon was the 664, which began on 23rd August 1936. This route linked Edgware with Paddington, travelling through Cricklewood, Willesden, Harlesden and Kensal Green, and workings were shared with Stonebridge. The route continued in this form until 2nd May 1956, when it became a Mon-Fri peak and Sat and Sun route, the 666 changing to a Mon-Fri all-day route on the same day. The 664 was withdrawn on 6th January 1959 and the 666 ran daily from the 7th.

Trolleybus operation came to a close on a snowy 2nd January 1962, when routes 645 and 666 ran for the last time. The depot was surplus to requirements and closed that night, crews being transferred to nearby Cricklewood and Edgware. The land at the rear was being used by this time to scrap the trolleybus fleet, a job undertaken by the contractor George Cohen. The depot was subsequently demolished and the site redeveloped.

Maximum vehicles operated:
October 1938: **645/664/666** – 38.
March 1946: **645/660/666** – 39.
May 1950: **645/664/666** – 39.
January 1959: **645** – 8. **666** – 12.

Colindale's N1 class 1585 turns at Cricklewood St Gabriel's Church. 645s turning here had to make a short detour from their route at Cricklewood Broadway, down Chichele Road, to turn in Walm Lane. *Denis Battams, 2RT2 Group*

HOLLOWAY (Highgate)

Holloway depot, situated between Holloway Road and Camden Road, was a huge LCC tram shed built in 1907 and accessed from either Pemberton Gardens or Pemberton Terrace. In view of its size it had three traversers during tram days. The vehicle capacity was 230. A shed was also provided here for two tower wagons, and another for a breakdown tender. Trolleybus operation commenced here on 6th March 1938, when new routes 609 (shared with Finchley) and 617 began, the 517 starting the next day. The 609 ran from Barnet to Moorgate via North Finchley, Highgate, Nags Head, Islington, City Road and Old Street. The 517 and 617 operated from North Finchley to the Holborn loop, following the same route as the 609 as far as the Nags Head, and then down the Caledonian Road to Kings Cross. This conversion was the first in which trolleybuses had been introduced near to the centre of London and the first to use the soon to be formidable Nags Head junction. New H1 class Leyland trolleybuses were the first to be drafted in for this conversion, along with some J2 AECs. The 517/617 allocation was short lived, however, as it was lost to Finchley in a reorganisation from 1st June 1938, although Holloway did resume operation later.

The next activity at Holloway was on 10th July 1938, when more new vehicles of AEC class J2 formed the bulk of the operation for new routes 513/613, 615 and 639. The 513/613 formed a U shaped service from Parliament Hill Fields to Hampstead Heath running via Kentish Town, Camden Town and Kings Cross, then the Holborn loop. The Hampstead Heath section was operated in a clockwise circle via Fleet Road and Agincourt Road, and crews were instructed to show 513 when departing Hampstead, and then change to 613 when leaving Parliament Hill Fields. The 513/613 operated an all-night service, which was not numbered until 1946. The 615 worked from Parliament Hill Fields to Moorgate via Kentish

Holloway Depot was a large LCC tram shed built in 1907. The new trolleybuses shared the shed with trams, until the latter's demise in 1952. Access was provided at either end of the shed, along with accommodation for two tower wagons and a breakdown vehicle. Also provided were a turntable and traverser for trolleybuses. Most of the fleet was out on the road when this view was taken in July 1952. *John Gillham*

EXTRA
609
611
513
613
615
517
617
627
537
637
639
653
671
679

Holloway depot had the longest route number blinds when three numbers planned pre-war, but not used, were included. At the other end of the scale, three depots operated just one route each: Sutton, Isleworth and Wandsworth. *Roy Makewell*

Town, Camden Town, Kings Cross, Pentonville Road, City Road and Old Street. The last of the new additions on this date, the 639, was another permutation of the same, running between Hampstead Heath and Moorgate, running through Chalk Farm, Mornington Crescent, Kings Cross and then following the 615 to Moorgate. All of these routes proved much busier during the summer months and Bank Holidays, when crowds would visit Hampstead Heath and Parliament Hill Fields to spend their leisure time.

The summer of 1938 disappeared and autumn had set in when the next new route appeared at Holloway on 16th October 1938. This was the 679, which ran from Ponders End (Waltham Cross on Sundays) to Smithfield, passing through Edmonton, Tottenham, Manor House, Nags Head, Holloway Road and Islington. From 14th December 1938, the Waltham Cross workings were operated Mon-Fri peak hours and Saturdays, with Edmonton contributing. The complete allocation was transferred to Edmonton from 5th February 1939. On the same day, Holloway received in return a share of route 627 from Edmonton. The 627 routeing was from Edmonton Town Hall to Tottenham Court Road, running via Tottenham, Manor House, Nags Head, Camden Town and Mornington Crescent. In May 1940, some Mon-Fri peak hour journeys were extended to Ponders End, and from 19th May 1954 it reached Waltham Cross on weekdays. A month went by before the next activity at Holloway. This was on 5th March 1939, when route 653 began running between Aldgate and Tottenham Court Road. This was a very busy service, connecting Whitechapel, Bethnal Green, Stamford Hill, Manor House, Nags Head, and Camden Town. Some sections of the route had a 3 minute headway, even on Sundays. K class Leylands had been delivered to Holloway by this time and were used for this conversion. As can be seen, Nags Head and Manor House were now extremely busy and complex junctions.

Holloway's entrance from Pemberton Gardens. The conduit tram track is still in place in this view although the trams have been gone for nearly ten years. *Norman Rayfield, 2RT2 Group*

The final conversion to affect Holloway had been delayed until 10th December 1939. This was the replacement of trams along Highgate Hill on route 11. The delay was caused by the negotiations to find a suitable turn at Highgate Village, which was finally resolved with a turn at South Grove. The new route 611 travelled from the Village through Highgate, Nags Head, Essex Road and City Road to Moorgate. No other trolleybuses were permitted to operate this route north beyond Archway as special braking was fitted to the L1 and J3s on the 611. In tram days, the 11 had a supplementary service on Sundays, the 11EX, which worked from Highgate Village to Essex Road, but on conversion the lack of turning facilities resulted in the 611 extras turning at Islington Green. On 27th July 1941, it was diverted to Baring Street, but the loadings were so poor that it was withdrawn on 26th October.

This proved to be the final tram to trolleybus conversion for Holloway, leaving tram routes 31, 33 and 35 still running through the Kingsway Subway to serve south London. They were scheduled to be replaced in the south London scheme, which was subsequently abandoned, and so they remained side by side with the trolleybuses until their replacement by buses in 1950 and 1952.

On 29th October 1941, the 609 was transferred to Finchley in exchange for that depot's workings on the 517/617. An interesting point regarding the depot run-in from routes 513, 613 and 615 is that they worked via Fortess Road. This road was not served by any trolleybus route and was wired strictly for depot workings, but passengers could be carried.

The access to Holloway depot from Monnery Road and Pemberton Terrace is seen here. The shed for the two tower wagons is on the right and a second access door is out of view to the right. *John Gillham*

The first London Transport prototype trolleybus, No.62, spent its early life at Fulwell depot but moved to Highgate when the Q1s arrived. It is seen at Aldgate while working the 653, its staircase window, as fitted to the LUT vehicles but no other London Transport trolleybuses, making it instantly identifiable.

X5 class No 1379, was specially designed for use through the Kingsway Subway. To facilitate the central loading platforms in the tunnel, the vehicle had to be built with an offside entrance. Despite trails through the tunnel in the early hours of 13th August 1939, it was never a success, and the vehicle entered normal service at Holloway until withdrawn in 1955. It is working here on the 627 in 1952. *Bus of Yesteryear*

Holloway operated many classes over the years including some short wheelbase B2 types and members of the C1, D3, F1, H1, J1, J2, J3, K1, K2, L1, L2, L3, M1, N1 and N2 classes.

Conversion to Routemasters came in three stages as follows: stage seven of the replacement programme, 19th July 1960, route 611; stage nine, 31st January 1961, routes 513/613, 615, 517/617, 639, 653; stage ten, 25th April 1961, routes 627 and 609. Route 609 continued as a trolleybus route with the Finchley allocation only. Highgate's 5-vehicle Sunday working was operated by new Routemasters showing 609 until the route was withdrawn completely with stage twelve of the conversion programme on 7th November 1961. Work as a bus garage continues.

Maximum vehicles operated:
April 1941: **611** – 15. **513/613** – 17. **609** – 21. **615** – 10. **627** – 26. **639** – 11. **653** – 50.
Mar 1946: **611** – 15. **513/613** – 18. **517/617** – 31. **615** – 10. **627** – 26. **639** – 11. **653** – 49.
May 1950: **611** – 18. **513/613** – 18. **517/617** – 31. **615** – 15. **627** – 26. **639** – 11. **653** – 49.
Jan 1959: **611** – 14. **513/613** – 15. **517/617** – 23. **609** – 5. **615** – 10. **627** – 20. **639** – 8. **653** – 51.

HOUNSLOW (Isleworth)

Hounslow was a former London United Tramways depot, situated in London Road and opened in July 1901. It was completely rebuilt for trolleybus operation and was unusual in that the depot had its offices and staff facilities in the centre of the building, with the vehicle storage areas either side. Its traverser and turntable were along the rear of the building. The depot had a capacity of 37 trolleybuses. C1 class vehicles were on hand to commence new route 657 on 27th October 1935, running between Hounslow and Shepherds Bush via Isleworth, Busch Corner, Kew, Brentford and Chiswick. It shared the wires with the new 667, introduced on the same day, from Busch Corner to Youngs Corner. The terminus at Hounslow was about half a mile further on than that used by the trams. The turn was constructed at the junction of Staines Road and Wellington Road, and was uniquely provided with a push button signal light for the conductor to press to halt the westbound traffic and allow vehicles to leave the stand and join the eastbound traffic. The route remained unchanged throughout its life, apart from some Bank Holiday extras worked to Hampton Court from Shepherds Bush and shared with Fulwell and Hanwell. Hounslow's involvement was discontinued in the 1950s. Some of the second batch of Q1 trolleybuses were allocated here in 1952 and, after their sale, they were replaced by K type Leylands.

The depot, along with Fulwell, was included in the final act of the conversion scheme, at stage fourteen on 8th May 1962. It was not required as a bus garage and therefore closed, with its staff moving to nearby Hounslow bus garage. The building is still in use and is now an Access self storage centre.

Maximum vehicles used:
October 1938: **657** – 21.
March 1946:   **657** – 23.
May 1950:   **657** – 27.
January 1959: **657** – 25.

The turntable and traverser in Hounslow depot. It is November 1935, and C1 class trolleybuses 151, 154 and 137 are brand new. The new 657 route has just replaced the trams on the 57, and the London Transport conversion scheme is under way.
LT Museum

Opposite top The new Hounslow depot was built on the site of the old LUT tram depot in London Road, Hounslow. It only ever operated one route, the 657, and the depot interior formed a U shape, with the office building in the centre.
LT Museum

Opposite When London Transport received the second batch of new Q1 trolleybuses in 1952, Isleworth received an allocation to replace its older vehicles. 1842 was a May delivery, and looks very smart here at work on the 657 early in its life. It was to see further service in San Sebastian, Spain from 1961.
Fred Reynolds

ILFORD

Ilford Council Tramways operated from their 1903-built depot in Ley Street and originally London Transport had thought it inadequate for conversion to trolleybuses. To make it suitable, a new side access had to be constructed in Perth Road and new docking facilities provided. This work was completed and new E1 class AEC trolleybuses were drafted in for the new services. The depot had a total capacity of 34 vehicles and a shed was provided for its own tower wagon.

New routes 691 and 693 commenced on 6th February 1938, the 691 from Barking Broadway to Barkingside via Ilford, working only Barkingside to Ilford on Mon-Fri evenings, and the 693 from Barking Broadway to Chadwell Heath via Ilford and Seven Kings. The 691 worked to Barking Broadway full time from 8th December 1938. Later, on 12th February 1938, route 692 began working on Saturdays pm from Chadwell Heath to Newbury Park, but it was withdrawn on 3rd December so as to provide a more frequent service on the 691.

As already stated, the depot was the recipient of trolleybuses destined for South Africa during the war. As a result the wiring arrangements inside the depot had to be changed to accommodate the SA class vehicles, as they had no traction batteries and could not be manoeuvred in the same way as the rest of the fleet.

On 10th November 1948, Ilford gained an allocation on the Mon-Sat route 695, which ran from Bow Church to Chadwell Heath. The Saturday workings were lost, however, on 10th November 1951, and the route was withdrawn ahead of the conversion scheme on 6th January 1959. There were rumours of a sale of the SA vehicles but nothing materialised. The depot was included in stage three of the conversion scheme on 18th August 1959. RT buses provided the replacements and, as Ilford depot was surplus to requirements, it closed and its staff were transferred to nearby bus garages. The depot buildings were demolished in May 2014.

Ilford Council trams worked from this depot in Ley Street and when the LPTB took over it was thought that it would not be suitable for trolleybus operation, but it lasted in use until the end of the routes it served. This view was taken on 19th May 1954 and Perth Road is on the left. *LT Museum*

Special thought had to be given to the wiring layout at Ilford, as the SA class trolleybuses could not be moved on batteries. SA1 1730 and SA3 1757 are parked in this mid-fifties view. *Norman Rayfield, 2RT2 Group*

Maximum vehicles used:

October 1938:	**691/2** – 19.	**693** – 11.		
April 1941:	**691** – 23.	**693** – 14.		
March 1946:	**691** – 25.	**693** – 14.		
May 1950:	**691** – 22.	**693** – 14.	**695** – 3.	
January 1959:	**691** – 20.	**693** – 14.		

The Barking to Barkingside 691 route was a 25 minute trip, passing Ilford depot on the way. All of the South African class vehicles operated from this base throughout their lives. SA1 No 1731 is followed by one of the hand operated electric milk floats which were then a common site in Britain. *John Boylett*

LEYTON (Lea Bridge)

The depot on this site in Lea Bridge Road had originally been built by the Lea Bridge, Leyton and Walthamstow Tramways Company in May 1889. The depot was taken over by Leyton Urban District Council in November 1905 and reconstructed for electric trams, re-opening in December 1906. The London County Council operated the service on Leyton's behalf from July 1921. When London Transport assumed control, they had not planned to use the depot for trolleybuses on a permanent basis; its use was planned as a stop gap measure whilst Hackney depot was being prepared. However, the lack of a convenient local turning point, and the speed at which new vehicles were being delivered all led to a change of heart. The depot had a new side entrance created in Westerham Road wired up to form a turning circle, which vehicles could use when terminating, standing on the depot forecourt. Route 661 terminated here, plus night staff trolleybuses.

The only trolleybuses to operate from Leyton were the K class Leylands, which started work on 11th June 1939, when routes 555 and 581 began operating. Route 555 was shared with Hackney from 10th December 1939 until April 1940, when Hackney took over the Mon-Fri workings. Walthamstow and Hackney worked route 581 until 8th May 1941, when Leyton replaced Walthamstow.

The Sunday service on the 581 was withdrawn from May 1940 until May 1944, when the Sunday work was resumed during the summer. It worked in this way

Leyton depot, later re-named Lea Bridge, remained largely untouched when trolleybuses took over in 1939. A new access was created in Westerham Road to enable vehicles to run through the depot without the need for a traverser. K class Leylands were the only classes to operate from here. *LT Museum*

until the winter of 1946, when the route became daily. During 1944, Leyton had small allocations on many other routes, namely the 623, 625, 661, 685 and 697. The odd workings on the 661 continued until 1948. Journeys on the 557 were also worked between November 1940 and April 1943.

Walthamstow greyhound stadium in Chingford Road was provided with a special service. Walthamstow depot operated this until 1940, when Leyton took over, having more spare capacity. The service worked a 12 minute headway using six vehicles between Leyton, Downsell Road and Chingford Mount starting after the evening peak and working until just after 11pm. The vehicles stood in Walthamstow depot forecourt during the meetings, and when working to the depot showed 'Station' with a white blank beneath, from the display for Burdett Road Station. This operated into the 1950s but did not survive the conversion to buses.

Leyton was the smallest depot on the London system and had a capacity of 33 trolleybuses. It was included in stage two of the conversion scheme on 14th April 1959, when RT buses were used to replace the trolleybuses. The depot was closed operationally, and its crews transferred to Leyton bus garage, although the depot remained open as a turning point for Bow's route 661, until it too was withdrawn on August 18th. Basic wiring arrangements remained in situ to facilitate WW and WH staff trolleybus turns until 26th April 1960. The building was eventually demolished in February 1999.

Maximum vehicles used:
April 1941:   **555** – 8. **581** – 30.
March 1946:   **555** – 6. **581** – 26. **661** – 3.
May 1950:   **581** – 25.
January 1959: **555** – 5. **581** – 14. Sunday workings consisted of only 5 vehicles.

Lea Bridge ceased operations on 14th April 1959 and K2 class 1335 waits to leave the depot for the last time. RT family buses are stored in rows to the left and right and the crews will move on to Leyton bus garage for their future work. *Denis Battams, 2RT2 Group*

POPLAR

Poplar Depot in Leven Road was opened by London County Council Tramways in August 1906. It was the last depot to be converted to trolleybuses before the conversions were halted by the Second World War. London Transport enlarged the building considerably by extending over the former permanent way yard at the rear. A traverser and turntable existed here.

Trolleybus operation began with L3 class vehicles on 9th June 1940 when routes 567 and 665 commenced, with the 565 the following day. The 567, which was shared with West Ham depot, worked from West Ham to Aldgate along the East India Dock Road and Commercial Road on Mon-Sat, being extended to Barking Broadway on Saturday evenings. This projection became all day from April 1942. On Sunday, the route ran from Poplar to Smithfield. The Barking journeys worked Mon-Fri from October 1941, and also on Sundays from 27th July 1941. There was another change on 13th April 1949, when in Mon-Fri peaks and on Sats the route worked to Smithfield. There were also workings of the route that ran from Smithfield to West India Docks Mon-Sat am peaks from October 1942.

The 665, also shared with West Ham, worked from Barking Broadway to Bloomsbury via Plaistow, Canning Town, Commercial Road and Aldgate, and worked an all-night service from Poplar to Bloomsbury, unnumbered until 1946. The 565 was jointly worked with West Ham, and ran in Mon-Sat peak hours from East Ham Town Hall to Holborn Circus via East India Dock Road, Commercial Road, Aldgate, Clerkenwell Road and a loop via Grays Inn Road in an anti-clockwise direction. This was extended to Barking from 23rd July 1941 and withdrawn on Saturdays on 9th April 1949. The route was withdrawn completely on 16th October 1956. Another new route, which again had a small number of workings from West Ham, was the 569. This commenced on 23rd July 1941, and linked Aldgate with Silvertown Station in Mon-Sat peak hours. It was extended

on 29th October 1941 to North Woolwich. The West Ham workings on this route ceased after April 1949. As can be seen from these route introductions, the service along the East India Dock Road and Commercial Road was an intense one serving many of the nearby docks, which were a regular target for German bombers in the Second World War. Poplar also had some workings on West Ham's route 669 starting late in the war and until 13th April 1949.

It should be noted that the Commercial Road services were all compiled on one time schedule, and generally Poplar and West Ham worked all routes.

The greyhound stadium in Nottingham Avenue was provided with trolleybuses running as extras between Plaistow Station and the Docks and this service was operated by Poplar and West Ham. By 1959, passenger numbers had dropped dramatically and for a depot with a capacity of 149 there was a maximum requirement of just 58 trolleybuses.

Trolleybus replacement took place on 11th November 1959 (first day of RMs) at stage four of the conversion scheme, when all trolleybuses at the depot were replaced and it became a bus garage. The large empty spaces were used to house the buses formerly garaged at nearby Athol Street from 11th May 1961 and for a while to store withdrawn SA class trolleybuses and, later, Q1 vehicles waiting for shipment from the nearby docks to a new life in Spain.

Work as a bus garage lasted until 2nd November 1985, when it was closed. The building still stands.

Maximum vehicles used:
April 1941:   **565/567/665** – 92.
March 1946:   **565/567/569/665** – 86.
May 1950:   **565/567/569/665** – 86.
January 1959: **567/569/665** – 58.

L3 class 1467 demonstrates the turntable at Poplar. A group of invited guests from Stockholm seemed to be impressed in this early post war view. The depot was used in the early sixties to store many of the Q1 trolleybuses whilst they were waiting for shipment to the nearby docks. *Mick Webber Collection*

STAMFORD HILL

The LCC opened the depot at Rookwood Road, Stamford Hill in 1907. When London Transport converted it to trolleybuses, it had a capacity of 97 vehicles and sheds for a tower wagon and breakdown lorry. It had a traverser but no turntable. The only allocation of trolleybuses here was of the K class Leylands, and they appeared on 5th February 1939 when route 647 commenced daily between Stamford Hill and London Docks, running via Dalston, Kingsland Road and Shoreditch. Existing route 649, operated by Edmonton, was extended south on this date to Liverpool Street daily, previously turning at Stamford Hill. Stamford Hill operated this on Mon-Fri until June 1939 and from then ran only special journeys and some Sunday workings. Stamford Hill also worked on Sundays from Wood Green to Liverpool Street from 12th May 1940 until April 13th 1949, the buses showing 'Extra'. The allocation books show this as being re-numbered 649A from 17th April. On 6th February 1939 new route 643 began operating from Wood Green to the Holborn loop Mon to Sats, passing through Tottenham, Stamford Hill, Dalston and Old Street. The route worked the loop in both directions until 7th April 1939, when the number 543 was adopted for the anti-clockwise workings. The 543/643 worked Mon-Sat only. Also on 6th February 1939, the 683 was introduced on Mon-Sat from Stamford Hill to Moorgate via Dalston, Balls Pond Road, Southgate Road and City Road. This became a Mon-Sat peak hours only route on 17th October 1956. An all-night service worked on the 543/643, unnumbered until 1946. The 683 was withdrawn on 6th January 1959.

The end of electric traction at Stamford Hill came on 18th July 1961, when all routes were replaced by Routemasters in stage eleven of the conversion scheme. Although closed on various occasions over the years, it continues as a bus garage.

Maximum vehicles used:
April 1941:   543/643 – 35. 647 – 25. 649 – 11. 683 – 12
March 1946:   543/643 – 35. 647 – 21. 649 – 11. 683 – 10.
May 1950:   543/643 – 35. 647 – 21. 649A – 15. 683 – 10.
January 1959:   543/643 – 30. 647 – 19. 649 – 3. 649A – 15.

A good view at Stamford Hill showing two traversers. A Routemaster, probably for driver training, can be seen in the background. The trolleybus on the left is showing a Charlton side blind. *John Gillham*

Stamford Hill operated K type Leylands throughout its time as a trolleybus depot. K2 class 1198 is nearest the camera and faces the traverser pit in this view taken near to the end of operations. *Norman Rayfield, 2RT2 Group*

STONEBRIDGE

Metropolitan Electric Tramways opened the depot off Harrow Road in Stonebridge Park in October 1906. It was a traditional tramway shed and when London Transport converted it to trolleybus operation it had a capacity of 86 vehicles. Trams were replaced here in one operation on 23rd August 1936. New routes 662, between Paddington Green and Sudbury, and 664 from Paddington Green to Edgware started on this date, using C2 and C3 class trolleybuses. Also on this date, a revised pattern of working was introduced for existing routes 660 and 666, which also operated from Stonebridge after conversion day. Route 666 had begun on 5th July 1936, working daily from Acton and Hendon depots. When Stonebridge began its allocation it became a Mon-Sat peak hours and Sunday pm route, although the Sunday working ceased on 5th May 1940, only to be reintroduced between 23rd April 1944 until 22nd October 1944 and then resumed on 6th May 1945. The Saturday work was withdrawn on 4th June 1949, followed by the Sunday operations on 16th October 1949, the route now being a Mon-Fri peak hour service only. The 660, working from Hammersmith to North Finchley, was shared with Finchley and Acton. A Mon-Fri am peak hour service, unnumbered, also operated between Paddington and Acton Market Place with some journeys

It is 1936, and this view of Stonebridge depot, facing the front, shows C2 class 277 on the left in the docking area, and sister vehicle 275 on the right over the pit. No traverser was provided here as turning facilities were available in the rear yard. *LT Museum*

extended to Bromyard Avenue. Many other extras were worked to Wembley for football matches and to greyhound racing. In later years some E1s worked from here and, after the C classes were withdrawn, they were replaced by members of the N class. Stonebridge also had an allocation on the 626 and 628 between 3rd January 1951 and 6th January 1959. The 664 was withdrawn on 6th January 1959.

Like Bexleyheath, Stonebridge had a wired circuit around the depot, which was used to train new trolleybus drivers in the training school located here. In early years some driver training took place between Wembley Hill Road and Sudbury. Stage thirteen of the conversion scheme saw Stonebridge enter the list of bus garages after operations on 2nd January 1962. It remained operational until final closure on 15th August 1981. The building remains in use as industrial units complete with a remaining traction standard.

Maximum vehicles used:
October 1938: **660/662/664/666** – 76.
March 1946:   **660/664/666** – 44. **662** – 34.
May 1950:   **660/664/666** – 50. (+4 for **660EX**) **662** – 33.
January 1959: **660** – 33. **662** – 31. **666** – 7.

This request stop in Harrow Road is the point for the crew change at Stonebridge depot. A Sudbury bound N2 on the 662 waits for the new crew as the other crew members make for the depot, and perhaps a cuppa in the canteen. *Terry Cooper Collection/Mick Webber*

SUTTON (Carshalton)

The South Metropolitan Electric Tramways and Lighting Company opened their tram depot in Westmead Road, Sutton, in 1906. London Transport took over in July 1933, and the open-top ancient-looking cars working there were an obvious target for early replacement. The Board had short wheelbase 60-seat B1 class trolleybuses on order to do that. The depot had a capacity of 51 trolleybuses, and had a traverser and turntable. Two tram routes, the 7 from Sutton to West Croydon and the 5 from West Croydon to Crystal Palace, were to be replaced by one route but because of the slow delivery of the new vehicles, the new route (numbered 654) was introduced on 8th December 1935 to run from Sutton to West Croydon only. At this stage, a few Diddlers from Fulwell were used to make up the numbers. Eventually, enough new B1s had been received and on 9th February 1936 the route was extended to Crystal Palace, where a new roundabout was installed to create a turning point at the top of Anerley Hill. Because of the gradient on the hill, these buses were fitted with coasting and run-back brakes to prevent vehicles running away in the case of a failure. The B1s were ideal for the route as several tight turns were encountered, which would have been more challenging for the longer 70-seat vehicles. Having said that, three 70-seat J3s, which were also fitted with the coasting and run-back brakes, were sent in from Holloway briefly in September 1958, when some of Sutton's vehicles had suffered flood damage. The new route was extended for a third of a mile beyond the former tram terminus at Benhill Avenue to a new turn at Sutton Green, and after local pressure the Board agreed to use specially designed traction poles along the High Street. These were of a silver-painted fluted design rather than the standard circular pole, with ball finial, painted Brunswick Green.

The South Met depot in Westmead Road was a small compact shed and, when converted to trolleybus operation, was able to accommodate 51 vehicles. This view in December 1936 shows the traverser and turntable and over the pits are B1 class numbers 66 and 76. *LT Museum*

If ever there was an area of stability on the London Transport trolleybus system, this was it. Sutton only ever operated the 654, and apart from special workings at Christmas on the 630 and extras for the Mitcham Fair, things stayed much the same throughout trolleybus operation. It was something of a backwater, being joined to the rest of the system only at West Croydon, where it met the 630. The 654 was used for experiments with radio-controlled frogs at Reeves Corner. Because the vehicles operated were the oldest in the fleet, it was no surprise when it was announced that it would be included in stage one of the replacement scheme. RT type buses were used, and the last trolleybuses ran on 3rd March 1959. Carshalton did not last long as a bus garage, closing on 29th January 1964, but the building survives as a self-storage centre. A plaque records its original use.

Maximum vehicles operated:
October 1938: **654** – 26
March 1946:   **654** – 28
May 1950:   **654** – 29.
January 1959: **654** – 26.

The end is near. Carshalton depot, as it was now called, is on the brink of becoming a bus garage and signs of the building work needed to achieve this aim are all around. *Norman Rayfield, 2RT2 Group*

WANDSWORTH

The London County Council rebuilt the tram depot in Jews Row in 1906. When London Transport prepared the depot for trolleybuses, an extra traverser with a turntable was installed to serve the four tracks set aside for the new vehicles and a capacity at this time of 24 vehicles was catered for, although this could have been increased to 28 if necessary. Route 612 began operations on 12th September 1937 using D3 class trolleybuses. The new route replaced the southern part of tram route 12, which continued to work from Wandsworth to The Borough and was scheduled to be replaced in full at a later date, when the depot was scheduled to be completely converted to trolleybuses. The 612 ran from Mitcham Fair Green to Battersea, Princes Head, where it turned in a clockwise loop via Battersea Park Road, Candahar Road and Cabul Road where the stand was on the offside of the road. This route also had a night service, unnumbered until 1946. This was the only route Wandsworth operated apart from some Bank Holiday extras on the 628 from 1938 to 1950 and a small allocation on the 630 on Mon-Sat peak hours from 19th April 1944 to 30th September 1950.

Wandsworth depot was the white elephant in the list of trolleybus depots. When part of tram route 12 became trolleybus route 612 in September 1937, it was intended as only the beginning of a full conversion. The Second World War intervened however, and when hostilities ceased in 1945, ideas about the remaining tram replacement had changed. Trolleybuses made their exit from here with the trams on 30th September 1950. *LT Museum*

Wandsworth's allocation of trolleybuses were of the D3 class. No.507 pokes its nose out of the depot in Marl Street in 1950. *Fred Ivey*

The complete conversion of the depot to trolleybuses never materialised. After the war, the plans drawn up in the 1930s for replacing the south London trams with trolleybuses had been abandoned in favour of motorbuses, and when the remaining trams at Wandsworth were withdrawn the opportunity to convert the whole depot to buses was taken. Trolleybus operation ceased on 30th September 1950, and the building was subsequently used as a bus garage until 11th July 1987.

After a period of closure, it reopened in April 1988 as a base for London Coaches and the round London sightseeing tour. The depot was never given a code in trolleybus days, although it became WD when in use as a bus garage.

Maximum vehicles used:
October 1938: **612 – 14.**
March 1946:   **612 – 14. 630 – 3.**
May 1950:   **612 – 16.**

The 612 never reached its full potential, as the remaining section of tram route 12 was converted to buses after the war. It was a victim of the tram to bus conversion in September 1950, when electric traction was ended at Wandsworth depot. D3 class 515 has passed under the Earlsfield railway bridge in Garratt Lane on 30th April 1950. *Norman Rayfield, 2RT2 Group*

WALTHAMSTOW

Walthamstow Urban District Council built their tram depot in Chingford Road and services commenced in June 1905. London Transport extended the shed at the front and rear, to give a capacity of 107 trolleybuses, and a traverser and turntable existed here. Services commenced initially with C3 class vehicles, but many other classes also worked from here, as listed below. Vital services for the workers in the Docks would be a main part of the depot's new routes.

The first route at Walthamstow was the 623 starting on 18th October 1936. This ran from Woodford to Manor House daily, via Forest Road, Ferry Lane and Seven Sisters Road, and bridged a gap in the previous tram service. The tram route 23 had terminated at the Ferry Boat Inn from Woodford, leaving the route along Ferry Lane to Tottenham unserved. Between February 1939 and May 1954, Wood Green also had a small allocation on this route. The next development here was on 17th January 1937, when the 685 began working from Walthamstow, Crooked Billet to Lea Bridge Road, Markhouse Road, daily. West Ham took the allocation on 12th September 1937 when the route was extended to Canning Town, and Walthamstow had no involvement at all from January 1938 to May 1940, other than special journeys between Crooked Billet and Lea Bridge Road. An allocation was resumed in November 1947. The route had some weekday journeys from Canning Town, Hermit Road to North Woolwich from May 1940, but Walthamstow never worked further than Silvertown Station. The next activity at Walthamstow was on 6th June 1937, when routes 687, 697 and 699 commenced operations. These were the Docks routes. The 687 ran from Chingford Mount to Docks via Hoe Street, Leyton, Thatched House, Forest Gate, West Ham and Freemasons Road. The 697 and 699 started at Chingford Mount and ran through Walthamstow, Leyton, Stratford and West Ham, where the two split; the 697 working via Balaam Street and Freemasons Road to the Docks, and the 699 via Greengate Street and Prince Regent Lane to the Docks. All these routes were jointly operated with West Ham. The 687 was cut back from Chingford Mount to Leyton on 11th June 1939 when the 557 was introduced. From 29th July 1942 there were peak-hour workings to Crooked Billet, and Walthamstow lost its allocation to the 687 during the war years apart from an odd Sunday journey. On 8th May 1938 the 625 began working between Wood Green and Woodford. The allocation was shared with Wood Green, and the route was extended to Winchmore Hill on Mon-Sats on 12th October. This extension became Mon-Sat peak hours only from 4th December 1940, and from 29th April 1950 the Saturday journeys to Winchmore Hill were withdrawn altogether. The last new routes to begin here were the 557 and 581 on 11th June 1939. The 557 from Chingford Mount to Liverpool Street ran daily via Walthamstow, Leyton, Clapton and Hackney, and the 581 from Woodford to Bloomsbury daily via Leyton, Clapton, Dalston and Islington. Leyton had a small allocation on the 557 between November 1940 until April 1943, and the 581 was shared with Hackney until May 1940, when Walthamstow lost its working on the route. Extras were worked on the nights of racing at Walthamstow dog track until 1940, when they were transferred to Leyton.

Classes operated were C1, C3, D2, E1, H1, J2, K1 and K2. The depot was involved in stages five and six of the conversion scheme on 2nd February and 26th April 1960, routes 557 and 685 being withdrawn in stage five, and the remainder in stage six. It became a bus garage until 23rd November 1991, when it was closed. It has since been demolished for new housing, although the original office building remains as a listed structure.

K1 No.1099 has not long been overhauled, and it stands at Canning Town. The busy 685 service was shared with West Ham.
L.H. Nicholson,
Transport Treasury

Walthamstow Council built this traditional tram shed in 1905. The separate shed for a tower wagon can be seen on the left. Further expansion, to enable Leyton to be closed, was not pursued. Many trams were scrapped here on open land at the rear. This view was taken in May 1954.
LT Museum

Maximum vehicles used:
October 1938: **623** – 15. **625** – 14. **687/697/699** – 45.
March 1946: **557** – 33. **623/625** – 36. **685** – 7. **697/699** – 31.
May 1950: **557** – 33. **623/625** – 35. **697/699** – 32.
January 1959: **557** – 30. **623/625** – 28. **697/699** – 27.

WEST HAM

The West Ham Corporation depot was in Greengate Street. It opened in October 1906 and was the largest of the Council tramways depots inherited by the LPTB. The depot had access at north and south ends of the building and the trolleybus capacity was 170. Extensive workshops also existed here and overhauls, repairs and repaints were carried out. The depot was extensively rebuilt to accommodate trolleybuses.

Trolleybus operation using the new E class AECs began on 6th June 1937, when the Mayor, Daisy Parsons, drove 622 on battery power in an opening ceremony. The new routes would provide transport for the thousands of Dock workers in the area as well as local services. New routes on this date were the 669, 687, 697 and 699. The 669 ran daily from Stratford Broadway to Canning Town and was extended on 6th February 1938 over roads previously unserved by trams to North Woolwich. The only other depot to have worked the 669 was Poplar, who worked a few journeys in late wartime. The 687 has been described on page 82. It had a shared allocation with Walthamstow until November 1947, when West Ham took full responsibility. From 5th May 1948 the Crooked Billet workings became all day on Mon-Fri, and from May 1950 these also worked on Sats and Suns. The other two routes introduced on 6th June were the 697 and 699, which were operated jointly with Walthamstow.

Route 685 from Crooked Billet to Lea Bridge Road, had been introduced on 17th January 1937, operated by Walthamstow, but when its southern terminus was extended to Canning Town on 12th September 1937, West Ham took over the whole allocation. Further extensions took place on 4th August 1938 in Mon-Sat peaks and Sat daytime to Victoria Docks, and in June 1939 on Mon-Sat peak hours, to Silvertown Station. Some journeys also worked to North Woolwich from Canning Town, Hermit Road Mon-Sat from May 1940. From 8th December 1940 the Sunday service was extended to Silvertown Station for approximately 2-3 hours during the afternoon. Also on the 12th September 1937, new route 689 commenced. This was a very local route, running daily from Stratford Broadway via West Ham Lane, Portway, Plashet Road, Plashet Grove, High Street North, Barking Road, Green Street and then back to Plashet Road and return to Stratford Broadway. This loop was operated in both directions with the same route number, but after much confusion, the anti-clockwise loop was renumbered 690 on 28th October 1937.

When Poplar became a trolleybus depot on 9th June 1940, West Ham played a part in operating new routes 565, 567 and 665. The 565 was withdrawn completely on 16th October 1956. The 569 began on 23rd July 1941, again operated with Poplar. West Ham's involvement in this route ceased in April 1949. Extra trolleybuses were needed for home football matches of West Ham at Upton Park. Wartime bomb damage was heavy here, and has been described in the wartime chapter. West Ham was second only to Bexleyheath in loss of trolleybuses through bombing.

The conversion of West Ham to Routemaster buses came in stage four of the conversion scheme on 10th November 1959, when routes 567 and 665 last ran. Stage five followed on 2nd February 1960 with the 669, 685 and 689/690 falling by the wayside, and stage six on 26th April 1960 when the final routes 687, 697 and 699 became history. Appropriately, trolleybus 622 performed the last rites. The building continued as a bus garage until 10th October 1992, when it closed. It has since been demolished, although the traffic office building survives. A residential street, Routemaster Close, now occupies part of the depot site.

Maximum vehicles used:

October 1938:	669 – 20. 685 – 31. 687/697/699 – 32. 689/690 – 15.
March 1946:	669 – 21. 685 – 35. 689/697/699 – 47. 689/690 – 15. 565/567/665 – 43.
May 1950:	669 – 41. 685 – 32. 687 – 22. 689/690 – 16. 697/699 – 28. 565/567/665 – 33.
January 1959:	669 – 39. 685 – 29. 687 – 21. 689/690 – 11. 697/699 – 27. 567/569/665 – 11.

It is 24th October 1959, and West Ham are playing Blackpool at Upton Park. M1 class 1547 turns from Green Street into the Barking Road on its circular route back to Stratford Broadway via High Street North and Plashet Grove on the 690 which, along with its clockwise partner 689, was a relatively quiet East End route except on occasions such as this. Plenty of pints will be bought in the Boleyn before and after the game. West Ham won the match 1-0. *LTPS*

85

WOOD GREEN

The former Metropolitan Electric Tramways depot in High Road, Wood Green, was opened for electric trams in July 1904, and when the LPTB converted it for trolleybuses it was extended over a former forecourt to give a much larger covered area. The depot had a traverser and turntable and a capacity of 108 trolleybuses, the first of which were of the H1 class. 8th May 1938 was the date routes 625, 629 and 641 commenced. The 625 was a daily route worked with Walthamstow. Wood Green did not operate this route on Sundays, apart from 5th February to 31st March 1940, when trolleybuses worked pm between Tottenham Hale and Wood Green. Their Saturday involvement ceased on 6th November 1948. From 1951, only a few Mon-Fri peak hour journeys were operated. The 625 worked between Becontree Avenue and Enfield on Christmas Days from 1939, and these journeys were also carried out early on Sundays in the war for munitions workers in the area. This extension was discontinued in March 1954. Route 629 worked daily from Enfield to Tottenham Court Road, serving Winchmore Hill, Wood Green, Manor House, Nags Head and Camden Town. The third new route was the 641 which linked Winchmore Hill with Moorgate travelling through Wood Green, Manor House, Green Lanes and City Road.

The MET depot at Wood Green was greatly extended for trolleybus working. Experimental new lighter fittings by the Ohio Brass Company were used here in 1938 as part of the overhead equipment, but were not a success. This view is on 29th May 1954.
LT Museum

Other routes involving Wood Green depot were the 623 and 627. The 623, a route mainly operated by Walthamstow, had a few journeys worked between March 1939 and May 1954. The 627 had commenced on 6th November 1938 from Edmonton depot. From 5th February 1939, Wood Green received a share, along with Holloway. The Wood Green allocation was a Mon-Sat working only. The small involvement in route 625 came to an end on 26th April 1960, when this was converted to buses. Vehicles running in from the north would de-pole and coast downhill under gravity, before turning right into the depot. In later years, K type Leylands were worked from here until conversion in 1961.

Wood Green's trolleybus days came to an end at stage ten of the replacement scheme, when routes 627 and 629 were withdrawn on 25th April 1961, and at stage twelve on 7th November 1961, when the 641 ceased to run. The building continues as a bus garage.

Maximum vehicles used:

October 1938:	**625** – 9.		**629** – 42.	**641** – 39.
March 1946:	**623/625** – 6.	**627** – 8.	**629** – 45.	**641** – 46.
May 1950:	**625** – 6.	**627** – 8.	**629** – 49.	**641** – 46.
January 1959:	**625** – 6.	**627** – 6.	**629** – 40.	**641** – 41.

The date is 23rd January 1947 and this view, taken from the pits, looks across the traverser turntable. Nearest the camera are two of Wood Green's large fleet of H1 buses, numbers 781 and 756. *LT Museum*

WORKS

London Transport carried out the overhaul of the trolleybus fleet at two main premises, situated at Fulwell depot and Charlton works. Partial overhauls were also carried out at West Ham works. Lesser works were carried out at Stonebridge (electrical) and, during the war, at Chiswick Tram Depot. Leyton also carried out a number of overhauls during the war when West Ham was bombed.

FULWELL WORKS

The London United Tramways built their impressive depot at Fulwell to include a repair and overhaul shop. This extensive facility was used to complete all work on the new trolleybus fleet from May 1931. When London Transport took over in 1933, and plans to expand the fleet were announced, Fulwell was set to continue its work as the fleet grew.

The works occupied half of the depot complex, and a traverser was provided along with a hoist (and later a second one) for lifting bodies. There were three main areas: the chassis overhaul area, the paint shop, and the body shop. Wiring access was provided from the Wellington Road and Stanley Road gates. Most overhauls for the fleet were carried out here in the pre-war years, and trolleybuses were dealt with roughly every thirty-eight months. Partial overhauls occurred at lesser periods and were sometimes done at the home depots. New trolleybuses were delivered here for pre-service checks.

In post-war years, when Charlton was also dealing with trolleybus overhauls, Fulwell looked after vehicles from Carshalton, Colindale, Edmonton, Fulwell, Hammersmith, Hanwell, Highgate, Isleworth, Stonebridge and Wood Green.

Overhauls here finished on 12th February 1961, when the final overhaul of Q1 1768 was completed, a vehicle which fittingly passed into preservation.

Although nowhere near as large as Charlton works, Fulwell works was much lighter and airy, and a much better environment in which to work. It was well equipped, and provided all that was needed for full overhauls. In this view some Q1s can be seen at the back awaiting their sale to Spain. *Terry Cooper Collection/Mick Webber*

Fulwell works in wartime, and Edmonton's K2 No.1164 receives attention. It is flanked by a Diddler on the left, and an SA on the right. The South African vehicles were usually dealt with at Charlton. *London Transport Museum*

Q1 1784 has finished its work at Isleworth, and stands by a hoist in Fulwell Works. It will soon be on its way to the docks to be shipped to Coruna in Spain where it will be converted to a single decker. *John Shearman*

CHARLTON WORKS

The Central Repair Depot, as it was known, was built by the London County Council tramways for the repair, overhaul and renovation of its tramcar fleet. The building occupied a seven-acre site at Charlton adjacent to the South Eastern and Chatham Railway branch line to Angerstein Wharf and was brought into use in May 1911. It was a mere 150 yards from the conduit tramway in the Woolwich Road. It was, in effect, a self-contained factory, and included all of the workshops and skills needed to maintain a vast tramcar fleet.

It was equipped with traversers, hoists, bodyshops, and included a blacksmith, foundry, woodworking shops, armature shop, machine shop, tinsmiths, as well as paintshops, and drying areas. It was also linked directly to the railway branch line, and had its own shunting engine. If the South London tram to trolleybus conversions had gone ahead, Charlton works would have been linked to the network in Woolwich Road, but that was not to be and throughout its time as a facility for overhauling trolleybuses, vehicles had to be towed here for overhaul.

The small overhaul facility at Bexley had been closed in 1938, and the equipment moved to Charlton, being installed there by the time of the outbreak of war. The ability of Charlton to pull its weight with trolleybus overhauls was severely tested during the war years, as the Ministry of Supply was putting increasing pressure on the works to produce more and more shell cases and components for the war effort. In post-war years, Charlton overhauled trolleybuses from Bexleyheath, Bow, Clapton, Finchley, Ilford, Lea Bridge, Poplar, Stamford Hill, Walthamstow and West Ham depots.

The final trolleybus overhaul at Charlton was on 25th June 1959, when N2 1669 was completed, and with a small ceremony and a round of applause another chapter in London's transport history was closed. It remained in use with various owners until it was finally demolished in 1992. The stub road leading to the entrance remains as a legacy, and is named Felltram Way, after Mr A.L.C. Fell, who was the Chief Officer of LCC Tramways when it was built.

Photographs of trolleybuses inside Charlton Works are rare, but in this view we have four. It is the summer of 1956 and an SA2 is on the far left next to L3 1454 which is in for a full overhaul. On the right is rebodied H1B No 799B, which is receiving a partial overhaul. The traverser pit is in the foreground. *John Aldridge Collection*

WEST HAM

The depot and works at West Ham were supplied by the Corporation to operate and service its tramcar fleet in the borough. When the LPTB took over and the trolleybus changeover had been implemented, the Board took advantage of the works facility that existed here to carry out partial overhauls and repaints.

The works was hit in a bombing raid in July 1944 and was out of action for several months, some work being transferred to Leyton depot. Local depots' trolleybuses were dealt with here, and partial overhauls continued until this process was discontinued as the end loomed nearer for the fleet. The last vehicle dealt with was L3 1409, and the works closed on 23rd December 1958.

West Ham works was bombed twice during the war, in March 1941 and July 1944. This scene is on 9th March 1941. Nearest the camera is H1 No.803 and in the distance are L3 No.1492 on the left and K2 No.1247. Being chassisless, 1492 was written off, but the other two were subsequently rebodied. *London Transport Museum*

The works at West Ham was the smallest of the three facilities and did not have the resources to carry out full overhauls. The leading vehicle in this view is E3C No.629C, rebodied by Northern Coachbuilders after war damage in 1944. *London Transport Museum*

Planning for the south London tram to trolleybus conversions had begun as early as 1937, but by the beginning of the war doubts were starting to surface as to whether it remained a good idea. Although the scheme was at an advanced planning stage and the replacement routes and depot conversions had been set out, it was not to be, and an announcement was made on 15th November 1946 stating that the remaining tramway network would be replaced by buses. The scheme started on 1st October 1950 and was completed in the early hours of 6th July 1952 when the last of the old trams ran in the capital.

The Board had calculated in 1945 that it needed 77 new trolleybuses to replace the 60 ageing Diddlers and the 17 of other types lost in the war due to enemy action and fire. The Ministry of War Transport agreed to this and London's first post-war order for trolleybuses was placed. Deliveries began in January 1948. The vehicles were designated class Q1, and were to have chassis by BUT (an amalgamation of AEC and Leyland) and bodywork by Metro-Cammell. The supporters of the trolleybus must have been heartened by this fact, but within a few months of the last new Q1 being delivered, plans were being drawn up regarding trolleybus replacement.

It had long been suggested that the life expectancy of a trolleybus was greater than that of a bus, but in a document dated April 1949, this was disputed: 'It is not sound to assume a longer economic life for trolleybuses than for buses. In practice, the life of both vehicles depends on the structural life of the body, and the design of modern vehicles of both types is the same' it claimed.

Sunny suburban Tolworth. Diddler No.41 is at the Red Lion in Tolworth and has not got far to go to reach the stand at Warren Drive by the by-pass. It is the early post war period and this bus would be withdrawn in 1949. *LCCTT*

A.B.B. Valentine, a Board member of the London Transport Executive set up to replace the LPTB at the beginning of 1948, sent out a 'Policy in regard to replacement of trolleybuses' on 2nd May 1949. The three main points of this document were: (a) to replace all trolleybuses with new trolleybuses; (b) to replace some of the trolleybuses with buses, and some with trolleybuses and (c) to replace the trolleybuses with buses. He discusses the fact that the main objections to trolleybuses were that they were limited to using wide roads free from sharp bends (a point surely open to debate), the fact that their termini often fell short of the main objective, the inability to pass each other, and the disruption caused by a power supply breakdown. The whole system was analysed, and out of a total of 1615 trolleybuses operated on Mondays to Fridays, it was shown that 1201 of them could be operated more satisfactorily as buses with amended routeing. It was then pointed out that to operate only the remaining 414 trolleybuses would be uneconomic. The last sentence of the document reads: 'Having regard to the foregoing it is considered that trolleybuses should be substituted by oil buses in total'. These points were all brought up in a subsequent meeting on 19th May, when the items regarding wide roads and sharp bends were disputed. It was also brought to attention that a trolleybus chassis requires less maintenance in later life than that of a motor bus. London was nevertheless on course to abandon the trolleybus.

The post-war Q1s were destined to outlast the youngest of the pre-war fleet by at least eight years and unless further new trolleybuses were ordered, the problem would arise as to where these new vehicles could serve out their time. The idea of a pocket of operation that would be self-contained was studied and, after looking at Bexley and Hanwell, the area chosen involved the routes from Fulwell and Hounslow depots: 601-605, and 657 and 667. It was calculated that 127 vehicles would be required to do this, including operational spares. Some work would be

The condition of the Brush bodied B2 trolleybuses was giving cause for concern after the war and they were destined to be withdrawn by the mid-fifties. No.124 was a November 1935 delivery and waits here at Holborn ready for its return trip to Hampstead Heath. An inspector waits ready with a bamboo pole, possibly taken from the 621 parked in front. The vehicle was withdrawn in 1952.
Fred Reynolds

needed at the Twickenham, Brentford and Hampton Court sub-stations regarding the extra load required for the new vehicles. As the current Q1 stock stood at 77, the recommendation, therefore, was for an order to be placed for a further 50 Q1 vehicles, which were estimated to cost £5,600 each. This recommendation was endorsed at the meeting of 13th February 1950. The additional trolleybuses would be used to replace the 33 B2s and 61-63, 378 and the 13 worst trolleybuses in the fleet.

The operating department of Trams and Trolleybuses was merged with Central Buses on 12th July 1950 under the banner of Central Road Services, with J.B. Burnell as Operating Manager, and the door was now open for closer integration of services; an integration that would not work in the favour of the trolleybus. At this stage, although it seems to have been decided that the trolleybuses would be replaced by buses, no actual programme had yet been discussed. The new bus on the drawing board, ultimately the Routemaster, was to be a 64-seat vehicle, and much debate hinged on the replacement strategy of this compared to a 70-seat trolleybus. A survey of trolleybus traffic came to the conclusion that a 4% increase in the number of vehicles required should suffice.

The meeting on November 21st 1951 sought to highlight a point made back in 1949, namely the failure of some trolleybus routes to reach the actual traffic objective. Paddington Green and Chadwell Heath were mentioned as examples, but there were other obvious candidates. The cost of rebuilding works at depots was also raised, and a figure of £900,000 was estimated at 1951 prices. Against this backdrop, deliveries of the second batch of Q1 trolleybuses began in May 1952, and all 50 were in stock by the following January.

The Q1 was a splendid looking vehicle. Its five bay construction gave it a more modern appearance and the 8 feet wide body gave just that extra bit of gangway room. No.1772 had been delivered in March 1948 and it stands at Wimbledon terminus in its early days prepared for the journey back to Teddington. *Fred Reynolds*

Opposite 1779 was the first Q1 to be delivered in January 1948. London Transport took the opportunity to photograph the vehicle extensively and these two interior views show the light and airy environment that greeted the passenger of the most modern trolleybuses the undertaking operated. *London Transport Museum*

The trolleybus replacement working party was appointed on 26th March 1952 to compile a report on present trolleybus routes and their replacement bus services. Their findings were quite detailed, covering all services except those operated by Fulwell and Isleworth. Some of the key proposals affecting the inner London terminals were new bus extensions of the 662 to London Bridge, the 627 projected over the 39 to Southfields, the 677 diverted to Cannon Street and on to West Norwood over route 48, and the 639 on to Greenwich over route 70. The outer London suggestions included extending the 698 over the 229 to Orpington, the 654 linked with the 186 to Woolwich, and the 662 on to Harrow via route 18. The report states that although trolleybus working expenses were lower than those of buses, the advantage would be lost when taking into account all of the other pluses that the bus had to offer. It was estimated that an extra 500 buses could be accommodated when all of the depots had been converted for bus operation. The report closes by saying 'the Executive have come to the conclusion that in principle, the present trolleybus fleet should be replaced by 64-seater oil buses of the type now being developed, beginning in the year 1957, and approval of the British Transport Commission is sought'.

TROLLEYBUS REPLACEMENT WORKING PARTY REPORT 1952
Summary of recommendations. No changes proposed to routes not listed below.

Routes 513/613 replaced by an extension of route 179 to Parliament Hill Fields via Farringdon Road and a new route between Holborn and Hampstead Heath via Grays Inn Road.

Route 555 extended to Waterloo with some reduction in 196 peak hour service between Waterloo and Kings Cross.

Route 581 replaced by strengthening of 38/38A and diversion of the 38A between Clapton Garage and Dalston.

Route 627 extended to Southfields to combine with route 39.

Route 630 extended in peak hours to Park Royal over route 12.

Route 639 extended to Greenwich to take up the Moorgate to London Bridge short workings on route 21 and part of route 70.

Route 654 combined with bus route 186 by extension from Crystal Palace to Woolwich. (Route 186 had only just been introduced as part of the tram conversion scheme.)

Route 655 combined with bus route 92 by extension from Hanwell to Southall and on to Wembley.

Route 662 absorbed into strengthened 18/18B services and extended from Sudbury to Edgware and from Paddington Green to London Bridge.

Route 677 diversion to be considered via Aldersgate Street and St Paul's to Cannon Street and extension to West Norwood in replacement of bus route 48.

Route 683 replaced by route 76 strengthened between Stamford Hill and Moorgate.

Route 691 to be extended 'into new development areas' north of Barkingside.

Route 698 combined with route 229 by extension to Orpington.

Some trolleybus routes were paralleled for all or almost all of their length by a bus route, so merging them with the bus network was often simply a matter of increasing the frequency of the buses. The 683 was among those included in the 1952 plans as, apart from a short stretch of route in Dalston, it followed the same roads as the 76. In the event, the 683 did not survive until the main conversion programme, being one of the casualties of the post-strike cuts in 1958. *Norman Rayfield, 2RT2 Group*

The combination of routes 655 and 92 was proposed to run between Hammersmith and Wembley via Brentford and Hanwell. Whether the peak hour extension to Clapham Junction would have survived is not known, but if so it seems very likely that the route would have operated in overlapping sections. *Norman Rayfield, 2RT2 Group*

On Sundays, the whole of route 662 was covered by the operation of route 18 (Edgware to London Bridge), so introducing the 18 between Edgware and Paddington Green on Mondays to Saturdays was a logical step. There was however a short-lived plan in 1962 to simply replace the trolleybus route with a 262. *Norman Rayfield, 2RT2 Group*

The office of the Engineering Superintendent had five meetings in July and August 1953 to compile a report on the future policy of repairs to trolleybus bodies and the general run-down of stores in view of the remaining life of the vehicles. Representatives from Charlton and Fulwell works were present. The scrapping programme was based on a maximum vehicle life of 21 years, and took into account the rehabilitation already carried out at Chiswick tram depot, and Charlton and Fulwell works in 1949 and 1950. It was summarised that the total numbers of trolleybuses to be withdrawn would be: 171 in 1957, 336 in 1958, 395 in 1959, 364 in 1960 and 371 in 1961.

Again, Fulwell and Isleworth and the 127 post war Q1s were not included in the scrapping plans. The Park Royal bodied vehicles, the E3 and N2 classes, were all now scheduled for withdrawal in 1957, along with the rebodied suffix A and C buses, despite extensive work having been carried out on these by Mann Egerton and West Ham works respectively. The suffix B rebodied vehicles were considered good enough to continue until 1960.

Special note was made of class C3, E1, E2, E3 and some D2 vehicles. These were the vehicles that were extensively rebuilt between 1949 and 1953. A complete list was supplied to representatives from Charlton and Fulwell, so that they could take this work into account when these trolleybuses next entered the works for overhaul. The condition of staircases and wheel boxes was highlighted, and it was decided that replacement was better than repair. It was shown that Charlton had already fitted new staircases to 165 vehicles, Fulwell 129, West Ham 26 and Chiswick 82, making a total of 402.

The engineers then went on to review the general body overhaul, and list the main items to be fully maintained. They included floor slatting, differential cowls, floor traps, platforms, staircase treads, grab rails, half drop windows and emergency window, lifeguards, screens, mirrors, body bolts, wings and roof walk. The operating mileage of a trolleybus was an average of 42,000 miles a year, and it was considered that a body overhaul within four years of the scrapping date should be undertaken. Interior and exterior painting should not be relaxed.

The unions were informed of the Executive's trolleybus replacement plans on 25th March 1954. The Routemaster programme was seen as crucial to trolleybus replacement and on 30th March 1954, A.A.M. Durrant informed an internal meeting that it would be 1957 before the new bus would become available. He expected the deliveries to be: 182 RMs in 1957, 374 in 1958, 288 in 1959 (when a batch of Routemaster Green Line coaches was also anticipated), 374 in 1960 and 374 in 1961. The conversion would therefore not be able to commence before the autumn of 1957.

Route 565 was an early casualty during the post war period. The jointly operated Poplar/West Ham route ran for the last time on 16th October 1956. West Ham's N2 class 1657 is seen at Holborn Circus working back to the depot. *Ron Wellings*

The public announcement of the replacement by diesel buses of the pre-war trolleybus fleet was made on Wednesday 28th April 1954. A letter in The Times of 5th May 1954 from Conservative MP Gerald Nabarro was among those that spoke out against the abandonment. Nabarro, a well-known figure at the time, stated that the London trolleybus fleet carried more passengers annually than the London Underground (747 million compared with 672 million) and pointed out that the high passenger capacity of the trolleybuses compared with diesel buses meant fewer large vehicles on the roads than would otherwise be the case. He also stated that electricity generation in Britain was about 50% of power station capacity and criticised the movement towards imported fuel and away from spare energy capacity at home. Referring to the smog that had killed 4000 Londoners in December 1952, he also stressed the significant health benefits of trolleybuses. An editorial in the London Evening News two days later referred to the Times letter: 'Most Londoners will agree with Mr Nabarro. The one valid criticism of trolleybuses in traffic is that they tend to get into convoys of three or four at a time ... but buses, though unimpeded by poles and wires, get into convoys too'. It went on to call a conversion from 70 seater trolleybuses to 64 seater buses at a time when usage was increasing 'a crazy change'.

There were a number of considerations determining the priorities in the trolleybus replacement programme. The London County Council had planned for a new extension to Cromwell Road to be open in the spring of 1957 and, as this affected the area around Hammersmith depot, it was thought wise to include that depot in the first stage of the scheme, but in view of the planned timing of the works and the expected availability of the first Routemasters, this was clearly not going to be realistic.

In a meeting that took place on 2nd June 1954, the date of the first stage was envisaged as 1st January 1958. It was felt that operation of buses and trolleybuses from the same depot should be avoided if possible and that the sequence of conversions should be: Bexley and Carshalton in January, Poplar and West Ham in April, West Ham again and Walthamstow in July and October, Walthamstow and Highgate in January 1959, followed by Clapton and Lea Bridge in April, Bow in July, Highgate in January 1960 and again with Edmonton in April, and Edmonton and Stamford Hill in July, and Wood Green in October. 1961 started out with Colindale, Stonebridge and Finchley in April, Colindale, Stonebridge and Ilford in July, Hanwell in October, and the final fifteenth stage was Hammersmith in January 1962. Envisaging that some new overhead work would be needed at Hammersmith, it may be that the committee thought it would be best to get as much use out of it as possible.

By the time of a meeting that took place on 13th July 1954, the dates had been shuffled. The Clapton/ Lea Bridge, and Bow stages, had dropped down the order to be replaced by Hammersmith and Hanwell, so perhaps there was hope these could be converted in time to avoid the new overhead work. It was stated that the east London routes would be dealt with early in the scheme, as it would enable the majority of the manually operated substations to be closed early on.

This letter appeared in The Times in May 1954 and gave another angle on the superiority of trolleybuses over buses.

LONDON TROLLEYBUSES

TO THE EDITOR OF THE TIMES

Sir,—As a window-cleaner in the Chelsea area, I have first-hand experience of the filth caused by diesel buses. There is one house I sometimes visit in Beaufort Street where, until a few years ago, the windows caused me little trouble; that is, when there were still trams on that street and no buses. Now there is a bus stop immediately outside the house, and the windows get covered in a greasy film, and are very difficult to clean.

Yours faithfully,

M. G. WALSH.

71, Henry Prince Estate, S.W.18.

By December 1954, the trolleybuses at Carshalton were causing concern, and costly repairs to the 60-seat vehicles were to be avoided if possible. It was therefore considered whether it would be possible to convert the depot using RT types in a preliminary stage late in 1955 along with Bexley if feasible. Carshalton B1 class No. 65 is on the stand at Crystal Palace. The driver will engage his coasting brake when he sets off down Anerley Hill on the return trip to Sutton. *Fred Reynolds*

The situation was clearly still very much unsettled at this stage in the proceedings. Meetings were convened on a regular basis, and the fact that firm delivery dates for the new Routemasters were still not forthcoming did not ease the matter. The early conversion of Carshalton and Bexley depots was discussed again on 15th November 1954 when it was said that from an engineering point of view this should not take place before July 1955, and then it would have to use surplus 56 seat RT type buses. The reason for the Ilford routes being held until the final conversion in this plan was that the non-standard but sound 8ft wide SA classes could not be transferred elsewhere to release older vehicles. Confirmation of the possible early conversion of Carshalton and Bexley was

The unique twin-steer trolleybus 1671 was among a number of one-offs withdrawn in 1955 following service cuts. Built by Leyland as a demonstrator, it was one of only two trolleybuses delivered to London Transport to have a single rear axle and was intended to reduce tyre scrub, but on 1671 at the expense of heavier steering. Its body had thick window pillars by the first and last side windows as shown in this photo. *Fred Reynolds*

eagerly sought by the electrical department as new equipment, with more on order, was due to be installed at the Anerley substation, and if Carshalton were to be included in an early stage this order would soon have to be cancelled. Only one week later the issue of early conversion of these two depots was still to the forefront. It was essential, it was argued, that if this conversion was to happen within the following seven months or so, building works must urgently be put in place. It had been agreed to increase the capacity at Carshalton to 60 vehicles and use it to relieve the overcrowded Sutton bus garage. Bexleyheath was to be increased from 80 to 84. The closure of Athol Street bus garage and integration with Poplar was also on the agenda. A new document showing yet another revised conversion programme was produced, this time showing the provisional early change at Bexley and Carshalton in 1955, followed by a further 13 stages between January 1958 and finishing in July 1961.

In the midst of all of this, the Fulwell and Isleworth 'pocket' of operation seemed to be working fine. Both batches of the Q1 vehicles won many friends in the area, although the newer trolleybuses did seem a bit wasted on the Kingston local routes when they clearly could have come into their own on more heavily trafficked trunk routes in other parts of the capital.

When 1955 arrived, minds had been changed yet again. A meeting on 3rd March noted that Bexleyheath and Carshalton would not now be a preliminary stage of the conversion but would be stage one, provisionally in July 1958. It was stated that plans for the depot changes had been prepared and were being examined. The matter of closures was raised again. The closure of Lea Bridge seemed to revolve around the canteen issue. Meal reliefs scheduled at Baker's Arms would incur extra time for walking to and from Leyton bus garage and therefore using local cafes should be considered. Colindale depot, it was agreed, was too small and should be either closed or enlarged. The other garages in the area were already 'overfull', and would not be able to accommodate the Colindale fleet. A new and larger garage at Edgware would be the answer but this 'did not appear likely in the foreseeable future'.

The recommendation, therefore, was to enlarge the covered area at Colindale. Isleworth was also a candidate for closure at this meeting, and an enquiry was made as to the possibility of Fulwell operating all of the routes in the area. This was dismissed as 'wholly uneconomic from a scheduling point of view' and the matter was dropped. Ilford depot also came under scrutiny, and although it was agreed that the depot was too small, no suggestions of closure were made.

The closures of Athol Street and Lea Bridge were recommended in October 1955 and the suggestion that Hammersmith should follow was made. Spare capacity was available at Shepherds Bush garage, and the narrowness of the Hammersmith site and restricted access did not lend itself to continual bus operation. A statement of financial savings to be made if this were to occur was suggested.

The subject of the new Cromwell Road extension at Hammersmith was also a key feature. As has been mentioned earlier, the idea of bringing forward the conversion of Hammersmith because of this was still clearly on the agenda. The new buses were still not on the horizon, and if this conversion were to be brought forward, the only possibility of replacement buses would be of existing 56-seat RT types. The possibility of using the stored Cravens bodied RTs was mentioned at this point, although there were also negotiations taking place for their sale at the time.

By the end of 1955, it had been decided that due to the fact that the new buses would not be available until late 1958, the conversion scheme would now start in January 1959 and that the whole scheme would be completed in three and a half years.

Although the first two Routemasters were in stock by the beginning of 1956, the production model still seemed a way off. In June of that year, a statement issued made the point that if the trolleybus replacement programme was to begin in January 1959, orders for the new vehicles must be placed by July 1956. Tenders had already been received for the new bus and the price of £4900 in 1953 had already increased to £5827 per vehicle in the three years that had elapsed. The cost of the conversion programme, estimated in 1953 as £9,195,000, had now risen to £10,453,000 in consequence.

In 1956, there were service cuts to trolleybus operations when the 565 was withdrawn and other routes were reduced. In February 1957, it was announced that the Routemaster deliveries would commence in 1958, when a total of 156 could be expected by the end of the year. It was then agreed that it would be prudent to allocate the first 20 of these to a trolleybus route to gain proper full time experience of service conditions, prior to the conversion scheme. It was proposed that Bexley route 698 would be used as a self contained service for this purpose, and in March yet another list of new dates was issued. This list comprised 14 stages from January 1959 to July 1962, and included the same sequence of depots. The pre-conversion trial of the new RMs on route 698 was re-thought at a new meeting in April. Carshalton was proposed instead, as it operated only one route, but this was rejected as it was thought more rigorous conditions could be used on a route that penetrated Central London. Route 611 was then selected for this purpose but also not proceeded with.

Planning for depot rebuilding was high on the list at this time, and in June 1957 a list was issued giving details of the depots and their planned start of works. Bexley and Carshalton were due to be started in January 1958, Clapton in April, Bow in July, Poplar and West Ham in October, Walthamstow in January 1959, Highgate in August, and Hanwell in November. None others were mentioned at this point.

The RM delivery programme was put back yet again and was on the list for discussion in December 1957. The decision was taken to allow the depot rebuilding to continue, and that when further information had been received as to the new bus deliveries a revised list of stages could be drawn up. The conversion to RM of one or more routes prior to the main programme would clearly have to be abandoned.

The Trolleybus Conversion Main Committee were obviously getting tired of the constant changing of position with regard to the new replacement buses, and it was clear that if the conversion scheme was to go ahead as planned, a solution would have to be found to move things forward. In the December 1957 meeting, it was noted that the Chief Financial Officer had been directed to make an investigation into the financial case for employing surplus RT family buses in the initial stages of the scheme. This had been put forward as early as 1955, when a surplus of RT types had first arisen, but had been dismissed at the time owing to the reduced seating capacity of 56 compared with the 64 seats of the new RM. The four depots involved in the first two stages did not, according to those present, pose many problems, but the larger depots in the next stages would be more of a challenge.

As 1958 dawned, the position with the new Routemasters was still far from clear. It was thought that enough of the new buses may be available to convert Carshalton in April 1959 and Bexley in May 1959, but this was by no means certain. A separate matter mentioned was the replacement bus route numbers. As not enough numbers up to 299 for the new bus routes would be available, it was confirmed that, where necessary, the trolleybus route numbers would continue to be used. However, 1958 turned out to be the year of a protracted London bus strike, following which nineteen Central Bus routes were completely withdrawn. The loss of these routes freed sufficient route numbers to enable the trolleybus replacement routes to be numbered in the existing Central Bus series and this was decided on in September 1958. Until then, documents for the first stage had been showing route numbers 654 and 696 as continuing in use after conversion to bus, but these were now amended to 154 and 96, the latter number having been among the nineteen freed up by the post-strike cuts.

The rear wheel spats on the C2 class vehicles gave them a very smart look and 202 is pictured at Craven Park on the 664. The route was withdrawn ahead of the conversion scheme in January 1959. *F.G. Reynolds*

Building work was now under way at some depots in preparation for the conversion programme which was still due to begin in the New Year. The position regarding replacement buses had now become urgent, and in a meeting dated 24th June 1958 the subject of using RT type buses was again at the top of the list. They were to be considered for the first four stages of the programme. The work at Bexley and Carshalton had advanced to the point where they would be available for oil buses in January 1959, but Clapton and Poplar were behind schedule and Bow and West Ham were likely to be two and three months late. Ilford depot once again came into the discussions and it was suggested that considerable savings could be made if it were to be closed after the conversion. With this in mind, it was considered wise to bring forward the changeover date at this depot, which at this time was scheduled for July 1962. Closure was again discussed regarding Colindale and it was agreed that financial appraisals should be considered regarding these points and a possible further staging programme, all to be arranged for presentation at a further meeting. The powers that be were well aware that under the Highways Act, three months notice had to be given when any services were to be abandoned and the date of January 1959 for the first stage was looming.

The fate of Ilford and Colindale depots was confirmed in August after financial considerations had been examined. Ilford was to be brought forward to stage three of the scheme and then closed with the staff being transferred to Seven Kings and Barking. In view of the close relationship between Colindale and the other depots in the North West division, and from the traffic viewpoint, earlier conversion could not be considered. Another report showed that it would not be advantageous to use RT buses instead of RMs in the early stages, and therefore a recommendation for this could not be made.

This must have frustrated those in charge of the conversion programme. They could not be guaranteed new buses when they wanted them, and yet the answer to their problems was being denied. All the time, the January 1959 date was getting uncomfortably close. Another report was commissioned to examine the arguments for and against the use of RT buses. Amidst all this, figures were published by the Executive showing that passenger numbers had declined 28.2% between autumn 1950 and 1958 on Central Road Services.

Labour difficulties at Park Royal works meant further delays of the RM, and at this time it was obviously felt that a decision had to be made about the imminent stage one of the scheme; RT type buses would be used. Regarding stage two, it was stated in December 1958 that deferring its date would depend on how much would have to be spent on the trolleybuses to keep them fit for service; as it was proposed to close Charlton works in mid-1959, this could have an effect on the issue. It was agreed that a delay of up to three months would probably be acceptable but if necessary surplus RT/RTL buses could be used. Alternative schedules were released for stage two providing for the use of either RMs or RTs, as the outcome was still undecided.

The sheet issued in January 1959 detailed 13 stages from March 1959 to January 1962 showed Ilford now included in stage three and confirmed the use of RTs for stage one. It also confirmed the closure of Lea Bridge, Ilford, Hammersmith and Colindale. The Committee had at last been given the green light to use surplus RT family buses rather than keep altering the conversion dates.

A subject to resurface in January 1959 was the fact that there were 17 surplus Q1 trolleybuses in the Fulwell and Isleworth area of operation. It was suggested

that another trolleybus route that may be convenient for operation from either of these depots should be reprieved and added to the south west 'pocket'. The only route that came into that category was the 655. It was discussed but due to the dead mileage for staff changeovers, the retention of wiring in Hanwell depot for turning, and having to keep open the Hanwell substation, it was rejected. The recommendation was not to retain the surplus trolleybuses. In February, the Committee decided that the financial effects should be considered for the conversion of the Fulwell and Isleworth routes excluded from the original plans.

Stage one took place on the night of 3rd March 1959, and at last the plan was in place. Overhauled RTs rolled out of Bexley and Carshalton on the replacement routes on the morning of the 4th. New Routemasters were being delivered and the first 184 of the production run would be in stock by the end of 1959. Most of these, however, did not start arriving until June, and there would therefore not be enough in stock to commence trolleybus replacement until stage four which was scheduled for November.

The 657 terminated at Shepherds Bush, where 1792 has just arrived in this view on 23rd April 1961. A Routemaster on the 628 replacement is about to overtake, but it will be just over another year before RMs take over the 657 and its passengers will have an older class of trolleybus to travel on before then. *Denis Battams, 2RT2 Group*

BUSES FOR TROLLEYBUSES

At the beginning of 1959, after extensive discussions on the advantages and disadvantages of using the RT family of buses for the conversion programme, the trolleybus abandonment scheme was about to be implemented. The dates for the first two stages, 1st March and 12th April 1959, had been modified in the light of an internal memorandum dated 21st January 1959. 'These dates are on Sundays' it stated, 'and in this respect follow the precedent of the Tram Conversion, when it was found helpful to introduce ex-tram drivers to wheel steering in the comparative quiet of Sunday operations'. It followed then, since all drivers were now familiar with 'wheel steering', that no such special provision was needed and that the dates of the conversions would fall in line with the 'standard timetable fortnight', which was calculated from Tuesday/Wednesday.

The process finally got under way on Tuesday 3rd March 1959, when Bexleyheath and Carshalton depots lost their trolleybus routes. On Wednesday 4th March, eighty-five RTs replaced ninety-five trolleybuses on routes 696/698 from BX and on route 654 from CN; twenty-five miles of overhead were abandoned.

A.E.Butler from London Transport was interviewed by Ray Colley in a BBC news programme at 6.15pm on the Tuesday of the conversion. Typical of the tame interviews of the time, the questions included: 'Did the job of replacement present many technical problems?' Mr Butler replied in the affirmative, as he did to the next question – 'Did he think the new services would be an improvement?' In defence of the trolleybuses he stated they had given good service for twenty-three years and that they had covered a million miles each.

However, in the aftermath of this first stage of the conversion programme the optimism of London Transport's official spokesman was not mirrored by sections of the travelling public. Robert Harley well remembers the teething troubles resulting from the abandonment of electric traction. On Saturday 28th February 1959, then a schoolboy living in Blackheath, he accompanied his father on a regular visit to Bexleyheath Broadway: 'We caught the 89 bus at the Brook Hotel, Shooters Hill Road and got off at Welling Corner to transfer to the trolleybus. The weather was sunny and unseasonably mild. We were greeted by the sight of yellow posters on the traction standards. They announced the imminent conversion of trolleybus route 696 to bus route 96.

'The 696s were very frequent on Saturday morning. It was often the case that, as we were boarding at Welling Corner, another trolley would appear behind us. The same splendid service operated in the opposite direction. Although there was a backstreet turning loop in Springfield Road, Welling, I cannot recall seeing any short workings; just about every vehicle appeared to be going to Woolwich, Parsons Hill in one direction or to Dartford Market Street in the other.

'What a contrast on Saturday, 7th March! The faithful 696 had departed and in its place were standard RT buses on route 96. The weather had turned cloudy with drizzle. When we alighted from the 89, we were confronted with a queue for the 96. Several people grumbled that they had been waiting ten minutes for a bus – a state of affairs unheard of with the trolleys. Eventually an LT inspector came over to placate the assembled crowd. The general consensus from the frustrated passengers was that they wanted the trolleybuses back.

On the second day of RTs on the replacement for trolleybus 696, RT 4243 passes under trolleybus overhead at Crayford with a 'yellow peril' notice on the trolleybus standard announcing the end of trolleybuses on the route. To sweeten the pill for passengers, newly overhauled RTs were used for this conversion.
Alan B Cross

Press notices for two of the conversions, stage one and stage ten.

Buses for Trolleybuses

STAGE 1

On March 4th new bus routes will be introduced, and some existing routes changed, to replace trolleybuses 654, 696 and 698. All buses will run daily except where shown.

NEW ROUTE 154 SUTTON GREEN - CRYSTAL PALACE covers the whole of the old trolleybus route 654 and runs on weekdays to Morden Station, via Rose Hill and St. Helier Ave.

ROUTE 157 EXTENDED to cover the section between Wallington and Crystal Palace.

ROUTE 64 EXTENDED to cover the section between West Croydon and Anerley on weekdays and continues to Elmers End Garage.

Replacing Trolleybus Route **654**

★   ★   ★

NEW ROUTE 96 WOOLWICH - DARTFORD covers the whole of the old trolleybus route 696 and continues during weekday rush hours to Victoria Way, Woolwich Road.

NEW ROUTE 195 covers the section between Woolwich and Bexleyheath and continues to Eltham via Bexley.

Replacing Trolleybus Route **696**

★   ★   ★

ROUTE 229 will be extended to cover the whole of the old trolleybus route 698 and continues during Monday–Friday rush hours to Victoria Way, Woolwich Road.

ROUTE 132 This circular route (Eltham, Bexleyheath, Bexley and Eltham) will run via Danson Road, and continue to Erith on Mondays to Fridays and on Saturday afternoons.

NEW ROUTE 177A will run on weekdays only between Woolwich and Abbey Wood Estate, via Plumstead.

Replacing Trolleybus Route **698**

ASK THE CONDUCTOR LOCALLY FOR A FREE LEAFLET

Buses for Trolleybuses

London's trolleybuses are more than 20 years old and each has travelled nearly a million miles. They are now being replaced by buses which can go anywhere and so will enable London Transport to give better service.

In North London trolleybuses 627, 629, 659 and 679 are to be withdrawn on April 26th. To take their place six new bus routes will be introduced and London Transport's new Routemaster buses will run on the new routes.

NEW ROUTE 127 DAILY VICTORIA — TRAFALGAR SQUARE — TOTTENHAM COURT ROAD — HOLLOWAY — MANOR HOUSE — TOTTENHAM — EDMONTON — WALTHAM CROSS. Buses on this route will run in two sections: Victoria—Edmonton Station (daily), and Tottenham Court Road—Waltham Cross (Mon. to Sat.).

Replacing Trolleybus Route **627**

NEW ROUTE 259 DAILY HOLBORN CIRCUS — KING'S CROSS — HOLLOWAY—MANOR HOUSE—TOTTENHAM — EDMONTON — WALTHAM CROSS. Buses on this route will run beyond Edmonton to Waltham Cross on Saturdays and Sundays .

Replacing Trolleybus Route **659**

NEW ROUTE 269 DAILY TOTTENHAM COURT ROAD — HOLLOWAY — MANOR HOUSE — WOOD GREEN — PALMERS GREEN — WINCHMORE HILL — ENFIELD.

Replacing Trolleybus Route **629**

NEW ROUTE 276 MON.—SAT. BRIXTON GARAGE — OVAL — VAUXHALL — ALBERT EMBANKMENT—LAMBETH PALACE ROAD—WESTMINSTER BRIDGE—PICCADILLY CIRCUS — OXFORD CIRCUS — GT. PORTLAND STREET — CAMDEN TOWN — HOLLOWAY — FINSBURY PARK—TOTTENHAM GARAGE. Buses on this route will run only between Charing Cross and Holloway or Tottenham Garage on Saturday mornings, and there will be no service after approximately 2.0 p.m. on Saturday afternoons.

Replacing Trolleybus Route **627**

NEW ROUTE 279 DAILY SMITHFIELD—ANGEL—HOLLOWAY—MANOR HOUSE'— TOTTENHAM — EDMONTON — WALTHAM CROSS. On Saturdays buses on this route will run also between Tottenham Garage, Waltham Cross and Flamstead End.

Replacing Trolleybus Route **679**

NEW ROUTE 279A MON.—FRI. TOTTENHAM HALE — CHESNUT ROAD — EDMONTON – WALTHAM CROSS—FLAMSTEAD END.

ASK THE CONDUCTOR FOR A FREE LEAFLET

'When the inspector parroted the party line of buses being more flexible, it was greeted with cries of derision. It was pointed out that buses on the 96 plied exactly the same route as their electric predecessors. Then someone suggested that, as the route 96 motor buses could hold fewer people, therefore logically, there should be more of them to cater for the same number of passengers. But where were they? There was a feeling the 'big' trolleybuses always had room for one more passenger, even when they were full!

'The situation was meant to be improved by new service 195, which went the long way round from Eltham to Woolwich. On that Saturday vehicles on the 195 appeared to be conspicuous by their absence. Eventually a 96 turned up, but there was little room to accommodate the entire queue. By this time the inspector had beaten a hasty retreat across the road. After about ten minutes at the stop and a further full 96 bus, we managed to find a seat. The conductor claimed there had been staff cuts, when the trolleys were abandoned. He also maintained that LT had not consulted fully with the workers about the changeover scheme. He suggested that the crews on route 229, the replacement for part of the 698, were so unhappy with the timings of meal breaks and shift changes, they had threatened to go on strike.'

In spite of London Transport assurances, travel patterns built up over decades were disrupted and the cut in service frequencies with smaller capacity vehicles had its effect. Basically, people knew that with trolleybuses in operation there would always be another one along in a minute. They were not capable of getting lost like normal buses! The trolleybus conversion programme had a psychological effect on potential passengers. The element of certainty of a fixed track transport system was removed.

The editor of the *Kentish Times* then joined the fray after having written to London Transport with similar complaints about the unsatisfactory situation. A reply from R.M. Robbins, Chief Public Relations Officer, came on 21st May. He stated: 'This changeover involved a complete recasting of the services. We had taken very careful observations of the passenger flows at all points beforehand'. After admitting that improvements to service frequencies would be dealt with, he promised changes to timings on replacement routes 96, 229 and 177A.

This letter from Broadway set the tone for future correspondence regarding perceived shortcomings of the abandonment programme. In fairness to the Executive, any new bus services were at the mercy of increasing traffic congestion. However, the Public Relations Office stressed time and again that 'careful consideration was given to the special traffic problems along the route to see what could be done, within the limits of economic and efficient operation, to give the buses when they took over a better chance of more regular running'. This justification by the people at London Transport headquarters rang hollow with many former trolleybus passengers, who felt they had been short changed by the service planners.

Over in north Surrey, home of the late lamented 654, Richard Sharples, MP for Sutton and Cheam, had written to the London Transport Executive complaining about the morning peak services of the new replacement buses. A reply, dated 7th May, from 55 Broadway pointed out that the matter was being addressed and that two extra journeys between 8am and 9am were being provided from 27th May. Remarks made to the MP by a constituent about the behaviour of LT inspectors were dismissed but they suggest staff may have been subjected to some complaints from passengers following the change.

In response to renewed discontent in the Sutton area, a letter was sent by London Transport to the *South London Suburban News* group on 31st August 1959. In answer to queries raised, the press office claimed it was not correct that diesel buses were more cramped, nor were they slower than trolleybuses – a criticism often aired when electric traction appeared to have an advantage tackling hills and steep gradients. Residents of Erith complained about buses not turning up, as well as being delayed, as they 'meandered off to Sidcup and Orpington'. After the dust had settled, an official review of the stage one conversion resulted in timetable amendments requiring three extra buses at Carshalton and four extra at Bexleyheath.

Trolleybus routes in east London were phased out in a year commencing with stage two in April 1959. In this area motor bus operation was well established serving the main trunk roads into the heart of the capital and therefore there was logic in the idea of augmenting and extending existing services to cover the demise of electric traction. There was also a strong economic case for the prolongation of replacing services into the City over streets previously banned to trolleybuses. Another very pressing concern was to tailor services to fit passenger demand, which had diminished in post war years. Contemporaneous with trolleybus abandonment was the inconvenience caused to passengers by the implementation of new one-way schemes, often taking services away from where passengers wanted them. London Transport stated that there was overcapacity on trolleybus routes and therefore it would have been uneconomic to maintain the status quo. It was quite apparent that passengers had been lost because of improvements in rail and tube services. Also, private car ownership was rising. The prolonged London bus strike in 1958 had also had its effect in driving away customers.

Stage two affected Clapton and Lea Bridge depots. The last full day of trolleybus operation was 14th April and ninety-nine buses replaced eighty-four trolleybuses. It was the last time there was to be such an increase of buses over trolleybuses. Lea Bridge Depot was closed and the crews moved to Leyton Garage to work on RTs; Clapton received an allocation of RTLs. Routes 555, 581 and 677 were withdrawn with the loss of 6.95 miles of overhead. The K type trolleybuses were moved on to other depots to replace older vehicles. The review of stage two concluded that some extra journeys were needed, and some others were not necessary. Had Routemasters been available for stage two, existing routes 38, 38A and 170 would have changed to a mixed allocation of RTLs and RMs to reflect their involvement in the replacement of routes 555 and 581.

Having completed the first two stages in just over five weeks, there was a short breathing space before the scheme moved to stage three on 18th August 1959, when 17½ miles of overhead were decommissioned. The depots involved were Bow (routes 661 and 663) and Ilford (routes 691 and 693). Ilford Depot was closed and the crews were transferred to Barking and Seven Kings garages, where they worked on RT buses. Bow received RTLs; its N1s were reallocated elsewhere. One hundred trolleybuses were replaced by 101 buses. The SA type trolleybuses formerly at Ilford were put into store at Edmonton, Stamford Hill and Poplar. They had been offered for sale; but when no bids were forthcoming, they were purchased by Cohen's for scrap.

In October 1959 the possibility of converting the Fulwell and Isleworth routes was considered again. At this stage it must be remembered that the intention was to retain these services, operated by post-war Q1 type trolleybuses, until these

vehicles became time expired. Moves had already been made to see if future buyers could be found for them. The LT Chairman confirmed the possibility of adding these two depots to the conversion scheme in April/May 1962.

Prior to stage four a meeting was held to discuss forthcoming events. It recommended: 'The short branch line to Smithfield is abandoned as far as the 567 routeing is concerned. It operates in peak hours only, is about 300 yards long and has negligible traffic value. The twenty-one journeys in the morning carry twenty-five passengers inward and the fourteen journeys in the evening carry twenty-seven people out!' The 567 actually ran daily.

Stage five was on the agenda for another working party, convened on 16th November 1959. Discussion centred on the layover time taken by trolleybuses at Wanstead Flats terminal. It was noted that nine trolleybuses per hour used this stand on Saturdays, but permission for motor buses was proving hard to obtain. It was decided it would therefore be prudent to reduce standing requirements at this point and possibly seek alternative locations. The 557 replacement route 257 was also on the agenda and a Sunday morning extension over route 35 to Brixton was put forward but not pursued.

Chingford Mount was a terminus that the Traffic Commissioner ruled needed to have a reduction in terminating buses. Route 557 has lost its trolleybuses and the 699 will soon follow. *C. Carter*

The date is 1st November 1959 and the 665 will be withdrawn on the 10th. L3 1444 will move on after this conversion and will end up seeing out its days at Fulwell at the very end of trolleybus operations. Gardiners Corner was a very busy trolleybus junction and the 665 has made its way from Bloomsbury through Aldgate. It will now travel through the East End to Barking with a journey time of just under an hour. *Denis Battams*

A significant event for London Transport occurred on 11th November, when stage four saw the new Routemaster buses replace trolleybus stock at Poplar and at West Ham. The latter depot was only partially converted and became the first LT establishment to operate both types of vehicle, albeit for only a short time. At the depots seventy-three buses replaced sixty-seven trolleybuses. The complex workings of routes 567, 569 and 665 were withdrawn and 6.2 miles of overhead made redundant. Clay Hall bus garage was closed and operations were transferred to Bow, which became the only former trolleybus depot to run RTWs.

A meeting on 16th December 1959 discussed stages five and six. It was noted that changes calculated to relieve the pressure on the stands at Chingford Mount and the Crooked Billett, as required by the Traffic Commissioner, would result in a reduction of vehicles using these terminal points from thirty-six to eleven and from twenty-eight to twelve respectively.

L3 class 1474, waiting at Barking, is working back to Poplar depot on route 567. L3s were the only allocation at Poplar and all moved on for further service when the east London routes were converted. The date is 7th June 1959. *Norman Rayfield, 2RT2 Group*

The new year of 1960 dawned and stage five occurred on 2nd February. It involved West Ham and Walthamstow routes 557, 669, 685, 689 and 690. The Traffic Commissioner insisted on a reduction of vehicles turning at Liverpool Street, therefore the 557 replacement bus 257 was extended to London Bridge during daytime operations. Overhead totalling 14.25 miles was lost in this conversion; 101 buses replaced 107 trolleybuses. Recent surveys on loadings for routes 669 and 685 had shown a dramatic reduction in passengers, and on these services forty-five buses replaced seventy-four trolleybuses as a direct result. Dual operation of diesel vehicles and electric traction continued at these two depots until the next stage of the scheme.

London Transport had begun to receive enquiries about the availability of the Q1s during the early part of 1960. In March the British Transport Commission finally gave LT permission to offer the vehicles for sale and, following this decision and before the end of the year, they had received firm offers for all the available trolleybuses. The sale was of 125 vehicles. It excluded 1768 (set aside for preservation) and 1841, which was non-standard, having been fitted with automatic acceleration.

At a meeting of the Trolleybus Conversion Traffic Sub-committee in March 1960, it was agreed that a new night bus service, numbered 299, would be introduced at stage six between Chingford Mount and the V & A Docks in replacement of the 699 staff journeys. Discussion also took place on the closure of Forest Gate Garage, whereby all route 25 workings would operate from West Ham. Another effect of the 1958 bus strike was an increase in spare capacity at depots and garages, enabling some rationalisation of premises in the conversion programme. In the same meeting stage seven was also mentioned. The closure of Hammersmith Depot as an operational unit meant that replacement buses would be stationed at Shepherds Bush Garage. New schedules dictated that route 630 replacement bus service 220 would operate in sections – West Croydon to Shepherds Bush, Tooting to Harlesden. It was also decided that the section of the 628 from Harlesden to Craven Park would not be replaced.

West Ham and Walthamstow bade farewell to their remaining trolleybuses at stage six on 26th April 1960. Twenty-three miles of overhead were declared redundant as routes 623, 625, 687, 697 and 699 perished. One hundred and four buses replaced ninety-eight trolleybuses. Forest Gate Garage was closed and its allocation of RTs was transferred to West Ham, Seven Kings and Upton Park. Historic trolleybus 622 was retained at West Ham long after its fellow class members had been withdrawn. In a fitting touch this vehicle, which had inaugurated services from West Ham Depot in 1937, was retained to perform the last rites.

Stage seven on 19th July brought two separate areas of trolleybus operation to an end. Hammersmith Depot lost routes 626, 628 and 630 and, as already mentioned, replacement buses worked from Shepherds Bush Garage. The Hammersmith building was destined to become home for the fleet of BEA coaches, which LT operated on behalf of the airline. Ironically, money still had to be spent on the depot to instal oil tanks for the coach operation. In north London route 611 was withdrawn, thus ending trolleybus service on Highgate Hill and its trolleybuses with special braking systems to prevent accidents on the steep gradient. In stage seven a further 13 miles of overhead became surplus to requirements; seventy-six buses replaced seventy-five trolleybuses. Highgate Depot received sixteen buses for the 611 replacement 271.

In October 1960 a meeting was held to discuss the new one way scheme for the Tottenham Court Road area proposed by the London Traffic Management Unit. Routes 627, 629 and 653 were deemed to stand in the way of the proposals, and although the 653 (February 1961) and the 627 (April 1961) were due to be abandoned in time for the scheme to take place, the 629 was not scheduled for replacement until stage twelve in November 1961. The aim was to bring forward the 629 to stage ten in April and the relevant departments were asked if this would present a problem.

It was decided that enough new Routemasters would be available and that the timetable for construction work at Wood Green Depot could be rearranged to accommodate them. The only small problem concerned route 641, which shared jointly compiled timetables with the 629, and was not destined to disappear until November 1961. Extra costs involved in splitting the conversion of the two routes between April and November were felt to be worth the money. The training of drivers was also considered and the end result was that the Committee agreed to advance the 629 to stage ten.

The sale of the Q1 trolleybuses was gathering pace and operators in Spain had snapped up the vehicles at a bargain price of £500 each. Invoices were being sent out to the new potential owners and Fulwell and Isleworth depots were now added to the end of the conversion scheme. Fulwell would inherit surplus L3s and Isleworth surplus K1s to finish their duties.

In 1960, 125 of the Q1 trolleybuses found buyers in Spain at £500 each – £250 less than RTLs were sold for in 1962. Early in 1961, 1810 is being loaded at London docks. Its eventual home would be in Santander, where it operated until 1972 and was converted into a snack bar in 1977. *John Shearman*

The *Daily Express* sent a question to the Public Relations men at 55 Broadway in October 1960. They wanted to know the comparable running costs between a bus and a trolleybus. The reply stated that a bus cost three shillings a mile, whereas a trolleybus cost three shillings and two pence. A bus averaged nineteen passengers per mile and a trolleybus twenty; therefore, the cost was 2d per passenger each. Later in the month, on 11th October, a press release informed the public that all-night bus routes 284 to 299 would be renumbered N84 to N99 from that date. This would enable LT to use the vacant numbers in the 200 series for trolleybus replacement services. The first daytime bus route to use an old night series number was the 286, introduced between Belmont and Raynes Park in October 1961, extended to Kingston with stage fourteen of the trolleybus conversion. The use of 286 was followed by the use of 292 and 293 in January 1962 at the time of stage thirteen. A minor point worth mentioning here is that trolleybus routes 604 and 605 were reduced in frequency at the time of the introduction of the 286, and from stage fourteen this route provided an alternative to trolleybus replacement route 285 as a link between Wimbledon and Kingston. At the end of the conversion scheme there were still route numbers available in the series below 280, i.e. 33, 136, 179, 222, 258, 262, 273 and 274.

The conversion programme moved across to west London for stage eight on 8th November 1960, the last conversion of the year. Hanwell was the only depot involved, losing the 607 and 655, and 18.9 miles of overhead. Ninety-five buses replaced a similar number of trolleybuses. For the only time throughout the conversion process a Q1 was the last vehicle to operate – 1812 being the final one home on the 607. This class had never been approved to work on the 655. As regards the fate of these splendid vehicles, the new year of 1961 opened with the announcement that the first shipment of twenty Q1s would leave for Spain on 20th January. Deliveries would continue until the whole 125 had been sent by 16th November.

The Trolleybus Conversion Committee met again on 11th January 1961. This time they pointed out that, as the 629 had been advanced to stage ten, this left stage twelve rather light, involving only sixty vehicles, whereas stage thirteen would encompass around 130. It was suggested that route 609 could be advanced from thirteen to twelve to compensate. This would result in eight miles of overhead and four substations being abandoned three months earlier than originally planned. This proposal was subsequently agreed.

A further meeting on 26th January considered stage ten. It was felt that the electrification of Eastern Region train services in the Enfield/Edmonton areas would affect loadings on the new replacement bus routes. Once the services were in operation, adjustments to the schedules might then have to be made. It was proposed to postpone tackling the problem of eight feet wide Routemaster buses in Victoria forecourt on new route 127 and the use of Victoria garage was suggested as a temporary solution. Another proposal was for a new route 258 to work from Clapham Junction to Tottenham via route 168 (which would be reduced in frequency) and then via Farringdon Road, Swinton Street to follow the route of the old 659. Replacement service 259 was to serve the Grays Inn part of the Holborn loop. However, the 258 was dropped from the scheme about three months before the conversion date, but a northward extension of the 168 did occur two stages later, when in November 1961 it was extended from Farringdon Street to Turnpike Lane over the old 621 route in order to supplement the 221 over this section.

New links between north and south London were claimed as one of the benefits of trolleybus replacement. These occurred with stage nine (new bus route 17 from North Finchley to Camberwell Green and route 45 extended from Farringdon Street to Hampstead Heath), stage ten (new bus route 276 between Finsbury Park and Streatham) and stage twelve (route 168 extension, as mentioned previously, and new route 141 between Winchmore Hill and Grove Park). Nobody could fault the theory behind these connections, but in practice growing traffic congestion in central London, plus LT timetabling arrangements, would combine to produce less than satisfactory results for the 'long distance' passenger. As regards the 141, in company with a number of lengthy London bus routes, the service was worked in sections and no single bus journey linked the two extremities of the route.

Stage nine took effect on 31st January 1961, when Highgate was the only depot to feature. It had operated Routemasters on the 271 since July 1960. Now came wholesale changes as routes 513/613, 517/617, 615, 639 and 653 were abandoned. Thirteen miles of overhead were lost; 111 buses replaced 107 trolleybuses. As regards electric traction, Highgate was left with only the 627 and Sunday workings on the 609.

Soon after this stage, Kenneth Robinson, MP for St Pancras North, on behalf of one of his constituents, wrote to complain about the replacement bus service from Parliament Hill Fields. Trolleybuses provided two early morning journeys from that point at 4.13am and 5.00am, and one from Kentish Town at 3.31am. These services were very poorly patronised and, according to LT, shortly before withdrawal of the trolleybuses, only two passengers used this facility. Thus, there was no economic case to continue with these particular workings. However, LT did point out that the first journey on replacement bus route 63 from Parliament Hill Fields was at 5.02am and from Kentish Town at 3.12am, 4.09am and 4.52am.

Kenneth Robinson was not the only Member of Parliament to have his eye on the trolleybus conversion scheme. In a ministerial statement on 1st February Ernest Marples, the Minister of Transport, apologised to the House for the delay in implementing a planned metropolitan one way traffic system. This he blamed on 'the difficulty about trolleybuses at the north end of Tottenham Court Road'. In a debate on 15th March, Ronald Russell MP for Wembley South, was told that a road widening scheme in the Harrow Road with the provision of pedestrian refuges had been deferred pending the withdrawal of trolleybuses.

A further meeting of the Committee occurred in March 1961 to review stage nine. It was thought that everything was going well, with only some areas of concern to be tackled. The service between North Finchley and Archway, which had been reduced in frequency since the changeover, was still 'overbussed'. New north to south facilities provided by the 45 and 63 extensions had not attracted much new traffic. All the new services were suffering from staff shortages, which were badly affecting London Transport at this time. A contributory factor was the retirement of staff at conversion time; some folk were wedded to electric traction and just didn't fancy swapping their trolleybus for a Routemaster!

The editor of the *Tottenham Herald* wrote to LT on 14th April 1961 to express concerns that the replacement bus route for the 659 would not operate to Waltham Cross on Monday to Friday. The reply, dated 18th April, listed the new route extensions available and stated that a traveller from Waltham Cross going south to King's Cross could make one change of bus or could transfer to the Piccadilly Line at Manor House.

On 25th April 1961, stage ten saw the removal of Highgate's last trolleybuses, when route 627 was withdrawn. Also involved at this time were the depots at Edmonton and Wood Green. A total of 141 Routemasters ousted 138 trolleybuses; 9.1 miles of overhead were abandoned. Since Highgate had now lost all electric traction vehicles, its Sunday only contribution to route 609, running alongside Finchley's trolleybuses, was now worked by RMs with the 609 route number added to indicator blinds. This stage finally removed trolleybuses from the Tottenham Court Road area, thus pleasing Transport Minister Mr Marples.

In May 1961 it was agreed that buses on route 243, which would replace the Holborn loop working of the 543/643, would operate in an anti-clockwise direction only. Although the practice of trolleybuses using the Holborn Loop streets – Clerkenwell Road, Grays Inn Road, Holborn, Charterhouse Street and Farringdon Road – was well established, it was felt that changes were now due. It was hoped the new arrangement would be less confusing for passengers and it had the further advantage of reducing the number of right hand turns for buses. It was also stated: 'The service round the loop will be concentrated on one set of stops instead of being divided between stops on each side of the road. This concentration will give greater frequency from the stops served and will avoid any passenger, requiring a through bus to beyond Stamford Hill, having to face a scheduled interval of 16 minutes in the peaks and 24 minutes in the middle of the day. No passenger will have to pay extra fares by reason of the new arrangements and the inconvenience to the passengers now using the clockwise portion of the present working will be small'.

The prospect of introducing a bus link from the Hertford Road, Edmonton area to the Southbury Road/Cambridge Road factories had to be abandoned due to the lack of turning facilities and staff amenities at Enfield. The Town Clerk of the Borough of Enfield wrote to complain about some of the replacement routes in stage ten. Letters had been received about the short working 269s at Winchmore Hill. This failure to serve Enfield was explained by late running and the need to maintain the service in the opposite direction. The lack of service between Edmonton and Waltham Cross was also raised, and the answer here was that the new 279A provided the link, which ran north from Tottenham Hale and was usually free of the delays caused by traffic further south.

The *Hackney Gazette* joined the debate after many people wrote to complain about long gaps caused by bunching of buses on the 253. In a reply, dated 1st June 1961, the case was made for the new schedules, which allowed for the route to be split in two sections – Aldgate to Finsbury Park, Mile End Gate to Tottenham Court Road. The system of freeing up buses on one part of the route from congestion at the other end, had worked initially at peak hours, but was now also being adversely affected by increasing traffic.

The conversion scheme moved on to stage eleven on 18th July, when Edmonton and Stamford Hill lost their trolleybuses. Routes 543/643, 647, 649 and 649A were withdrawn along with 18.2 miles of overhead. Ninety-three buses replaced eighty-eight trolleybuses. The turn at London Docks in The Highway was forbidden by the police for the new buses and a new turn in Cable Street was selected.

The *Palmers Green Gazette* wrote to London Transport in July. The focus was again on the unsatisfactory service offered by route 269. The Public Relations Office reply on 24th July stated the obvious. Traffic congestion was a serious problem, but the underlying cause was lack of staff. It was alleged that Wood Green Garage lacked a fifth of the drivers needed for a full service.

On 2nd October 1961, the South Division of Central Road Services held a meeting regarding the forthcoming Fulwell and Isleworth trolleybus conversions. Since the Q1s had now been sold, the path was clear to sweep away the whole fleet, and at this fairly late stage no firm plans had yet been implemented. It was thought the Kingston area services 'would present little scope for major route alteration'. The 604/605 stand at Wimbledon appeared to be a problem. 'It couldn't be assumed that the authorities would allow the present turning circle for bus operation'. The other stand in St George's Road, used by the 155, was subject to car parking problems. A suggested solution was that the 155, being parallel to the Northern Line between Kennington and South Wimbledon, could be curtailed at Clapham Common. The 604/605 replacement could then be extended to the same terminus. Prolonging the route to Brixton Garage via Tooting, by way of route 57, was also discussed. It was agreed that loadings would be taken on route 603, with the possibility of withdrawing it in favour of extra workings on the 601. Checks would also be made on passenger numbers using the 602 between Victoria Road and Portsmouth Road.

Meetings abounded at this time and on 30th October discussions centred on stage thirteen. Sunday services of routes 645/660/666 were highlighted, as it was felt that they were 'seriously out of line'. Apparently, the Sunday evening services were more than double those of Monday to Friday, and almost double those provided for Saturday. In addition, the Sunday workings at Stonebridge, Colindale and Finchley were exceptionally high. At this point it was envisaged that route 662 would be replaced by a combination of the 18B and new routes 262 between Sudbury and London Bridge (Paddington Green evening journeys). A 262A from Harlesden (or Acton in peak hours) to Paddington Green would replace the 660 workings between these points. The 18 service between Edgware Station and Wembley Empire Pool would be renumbered 18A. Route 268 was to have been extended from Willesden Junction to Sudbury or Alperton. Recasting of the plans saw the 268 extension dropped, the 262 subsumed into an augmented 18 route and the 262A become the 293.

On 7th November 1961, stage twelve was put into effect. Trolleybuses were finally evicted from Wood Green Depot and a start was made at Finchley. Routes 521/621, 609 and 641 were withdrawn and the overhead shrunk by another 27.1 miles. Ninety-four trolleybuses were replaced by ninety Routemasters. Among the latter the new 72-seat RMLs were used on 609 replacement route 104.

The penultimate stage thirteen took place amid fallen snow on 2nd January 1962. Stonebridge, Finchley and Colindale were the depots concerned and the routes involved were the 645, 660, 662 and 666, plus the rush hour extras from Acton Vale to Paddington, worked by Stonebridge. The largest loss of overhead so far, this stage claimed 29.37 miles, and 108 buses took over from 109 trolleybuses. Colindale Depot, which supplied 23 scheduled workings, was closed and crews moved to Cricklewood and Edgware garages. The 'unsatisfactory' terminals at Canons Park and Edgware were eliminated by extending the new bus routes to Stanmore Station and Edgware Station respectively.

London Transport issued an interesting internal document following this stage. It showed that the cost of removing 2,500 traction standards, at £8 2s 6d each, was £23,968 15s 0d; removal of 28^{1}/$_{3}$ miles of overhead, at £94 15s 0d per mile, was £2,684 11s 0d. The scrap value of the poles, at £3 each, amounted to £8,850 and the overhead to a massive £23,950 6s, which resulted in a net payment to the Executive of £6,247!

Complaints about the late running of route 269 surfaced again on 11th April 1962, when the PR Department replied to a letter from the *Enfield Gazette*. It was stated: 'In the case of the 629, on six typical days in March 1961, a total of 168 trolleybuses running towards Enfield were five or more minutes late at Wood Green Station; on the corresponding six days last month (March 1962), this figure on the 269 had been reduced to fifty-seven'.

There remained one stage to complete and preparations were in place for celebrations to mark the end of London's trolleybuses. These festivities are well documented; the weather was kind for the event. The last full operating day of electric traction was 8th May 1962, just one week short of thirty-one years, since the first trolleybus had operated for the London United Tramways. Fulwell and Isleworth routes 601, 602, 603, 604, 605, 657 and 667 were withdrawn and the last 33.15 miles of overhead fell into disuse. Isleworth Depot closed after the final 657 had arrived and the crews would start their next shifts at Hounslow Garage. Eighty-nine buses had taken the place of ninety-one trolleybuses. On 9th May 1962, for the first time since 1901, London was now without any electric street transport.

Many groups and intervals had argued against the changeover. Since there was a good case to suspect that diesel fumes could contribute to lung cancer, the mass abandonment of the clean, noiseless and quick trolleybus was regarded as a retrograde step. Another telling argument was that diesel buses ran on imported fuel, whereas their electric counterparts used home grown energy. However, after the furore died down, one was left with the impression that the trolleybus was only ever intended as a stop gap measure to make good use of the former tramway electrical infrastructure.

The conversion scheme was a costly operation, but in general it succeeded, bearing in mind the resources needed to implement the changes. Nothing as large and as complex as this scheme was ever going to pass off without a hitch, but most problems were eventually ironed out and London settled into life without the trolleybus.

Stage 1
March 3rd/4th 1959
Depots: Carshalton and Bexleyheath

Route 654 Crystal Palace to Sutton was directly replaced by new 154, with a Mon to Sat extension to Morden, and an extension of the 157 from Wallington to Crystal Palace.

Route 696 Dartford to Woolwich was directly replaced by new 96 with rush hours extension to Charlton, Victoria Way, and also by new 195 Eltham to Woolwich.

Route 698 Bexleyheath to Woolwich was replaced by extension of the 229 from Bexleyheath to Woolwich via Erith and the 132 from Bexleyheath to Erith.

Stage 1 was a simple scheme that maintained all the journeys that had been possible with the trolleybus routes and gave some new connections. The replacement schedules were however in need of some revision later in the year to rectify some shortcomings. The 96 still serves the same Woolwich to Dartford route over 55 years later, but with a non-stop projection to Bluewater.

B1 class 66 stands at the stop at Carshalton depot on 31st August 1958. The 654 provided a useful link to the shopping facilities in Croydon from both the east and west. *Norman Rayfield, 2RT2 Group*

Shortly after the war, an experiment was carried out with a radio controlled point frog. Three trolleybuses were equipped with transmitters for this purpose, the vehicles being 66, 70 and 88. The aerial fitted to number 88 can be seen here in the shape of a bar in front of the trolley poles. The view is at Anerley in 1953. *Fred Reynolds*

The 696 was, and (as the 96) remains, a major trunk route in south-east London. H1 class 800 climbs out of Dartford on 31st August 1958 on its way to Woolwich, a journey scheduled to take forty-six minutes. *Norman Rayfield, 2RT2 Group*

Cobblestones and covered over tram lines still dominate Beresford Square in Woolwich in this mid-fifties view. D2 class 474 on the 696 has just set out for Dartford. The Bexley routes played a big part in moving workers from Woolwich Arsenal in the war years.

The crew have just left D2 417 to visit the facilities. The vehicle is parked by Dartford library and looks as though it has not long left Charlton works after overhaul. It remained at Bexleyheath depot until the end of operations in March 1959. *Fred Ivey*

The old Woolwich Ferry entrance is on the left in this view taken in March 1959 on a rather dreary day. Trolleybus 405 had its body destroyed in June 1944 and was subsequently rebodied by East Lancs in March 1946, being renumbered 405B. *Alan Cross*

Stage 2
April 14th/15th 1959
Depots Clapton and Lea Bridge.

Route 555 Bloomsbury to Leyton and Woodford was replaced by extension of 170 from Hackney to Leyton

Route 581 Bloomsbury to Woodford was replaced by existing bus route 38A (Victoria to Loughton) re-routed in Hackney via the 581. Service on 38 and 38A strengthened.

Route 677 Smithfield to West India Docks was directly replaced by new 277 with an extension to Cubitt Town.

Lea Bridge depot was closed, but route 661, worked by Bow, continued to turn there until stage 3.

Stage 2 also maintained all the journeys that had been possible with the trolleybuses. Route 38A, which already largely paralleled the whole of route 581, probably suffered more from traffic delays than the 581 in view of its greater length.

K2 class 1255 is working the peak hour extension to Leyton Downsell Road in this view on route 555 in Leyton High Road. The K1 and K2 class buses differed only in electrical equipment, the K1s having Metrovick and the K2s English Electric. The 555, 557 and 581 provided a high level of service along the Lea Bridge Road, indeed an over-generous provision that contributed to the fact that these were among the biggest loss-makers on the trolleybus network.

Bloomsbury is the setting for K2 1345 working from Lea Bridge depot as it departs for Woodford on the 581 with Red Lion Square, the terminus of routes 555, 581 and 665, in the background. The date is 5th April 1959 and there are just ten days to go before the route passes into history. *Denis Battams, 2RT2 Group*

In a scene now unrecognisable following the massive redevelopment of the Docklands area in the 1980s and 1990s, K1 1297 is on the 677 at Ming Street near to West India Docks on a grey day in February 1959. *Denis Battams, 2RT2 Group*

It is 22nd February 1959 at West India Docks terminus, and Clapton's K1 1294 waits for departure time. The replacement bus service will be extended from here to Cubitt Town by way of West Ferry Road. *Norman Rayfield, 2RT2 Group*

K1 class 1299 passes the end of Farringdon Road at Clerkenwell on route 555, as a man struggles with a hand cart. An L3 can be seen behind on the rather busier 665 in the first phase of its journey from Bloomsbury to Barking. *Denis Battams, 2RT2 Group*

It is 5th April 1959 and K1 1150 has just left the stand at Woodford on the soon to be withdrawn 581 for its trip to Bloomsbury. The sign on the right for Regent petrol has also now passed into the history books. *Denis Battams, 2RT2 Group*

The fish bar and barber shop are typical of the small businesses that existed in their hundreds in the East End of London and this view is near West India Docks on 22nd February 1959. K2 1306 was allocated to Clapton. Special early morning journeys were provided on the 677 for Smithfield market. *Norman Rayfield, 2RT2 Group*

Stage 3
18th/19th August 1959
Depots: Ilford and Bow

Route 661 Aldgate to Lea Bridge was replaced by new 26 Aldgate to Leyton.

Route 663 Aldgate to Chadwell Heath was replaced between Aldgate and Stratford by new bus routes 26 (Aldgate to Leyton) and 32 (Victoria to Wanstead), new bus route 169A Bow Church to Barkingside) between Bow and Ilford and new bus route 193 (see 693) between Ilford and Chadwell Heath. There was also a strengthened service on existing route 25.

A mobile café provides sustenance for passers-by in this view near Whipps Cross. The trolleybus is N1 class 1613 from Bow and it is on a short working to Whipps Cross on 13th May 1959. Routes 661 and 663 ran together from Aldgate to Stratford and provided a high frequency of service along the Bow Road. *Denis Battams, 2RT2 Group*

Route 691 Barking to Barkingside was directly replaced by new 169.

Route 693 Barking to Chadwell Heath was directly replaced by new 193 with an extension on Sat afternoons to Hornchurch.

Ilford depot was closed.

Apart from the complicated set of changes in respect of route 663, the new routes were direct replacements for the trolleybus services with two extensions. Anyone who had been used to travelling from Chadwell Heath to Aldgate by 663 trolleybus now found they had to change at Ilford onto a 25 bus.

It is April 1958 in Ley Street, Ilford, and 899 is an H1 class trolleybus which was allocated to Ilford depot for nearly two years. The more normal fare for the 693 is represented by SA3 1760, which passes in the other direction about to turn into Hainault Street on a diversion because of work on the bridge at Ilford station. *Denis Battams, 2RT2 Group*

Bow operated N class trolleybuses throughout its existence as a trolleybus depot. 1608 was an N1 vehicle and Stratford Broadway is the setting for this 13th August 1959 view on the 663. *Denis Battams, 2RT2 Group*

On home territory in Ilford is SA1 1731 on its way to Chadwell Heath on 13th August 1959. The front adverts were one of several designs employed by London Transport to occupy the spaces when advertisers were sparse. *Norman Rayfield, 2RT2 Group*

SA3 class number 1760 passes the Newbury Park turn in Buntingbridge Road on the 691. It is 13th August 1959 and within a week the Ilford trolleybus routes will be all but a memory. *Denis Battams, 2RT2 Group*

Stage 4
10th/11th November 1959.
Depots: West Ham and Poplar.

Route 567 Smithfield to Barking via Aldgate and Route 665 Bloomsbury to Barking via Aldgate were replaced by new route 5 Bloomsbury to Barking Garage. A Mon-Fri route 5A was introduced to run between Clerkenwell Green and West India Dock. A Monday to Saturday route 238 was also introduced over the section from Canning Town to Barking, continuing on to Becontree in replacement of bus route 23B. The night service on route 665 (Bloomsbury to Poplar) was replaced by new night bus route 284, extended from Bloomsbury to Trafalgar Square. One early morning journey worked to Barking Broadway.

Route 569 Aldgate to North Woolwich was replaced by new route 48 extended from Aldgate to Waterloo.

As a direct result of this stage, Clay Hall and, shortly after (May 1961), Athol Street bus garages were closed.

The replacement of routes 567 and 665 by a single bus route, with the 5A basically being a short working of the 5, was a result of the very small difference between the 567 and the 665. The 567 followed a short stub off Clerkenwell Road to reach Smithfield. The 569's replacement, over its original section, suffered badly from traffic delays when extended to Waterloo, a downside of London Transport's desire to provide new connections with the absorption of the trolleybus network into the bus network.

It is deserted at Smithfield in this early fifties view of P1 class 1698 on the 567. The vehicle later moved to Edmonton and then Hammersmith. The Barking Road routes were closely inter-worked by Poplar and West Ham to provide a high frequency of service.
C. Carter

The Greengate at West Ham was an impressive junction on the Barking Road. The wires shown from left to right were for the 699 which crossed the main road at this point. West Ham depot runs were also catered for, the depot being situated off to the left. L3 1447 was photographed on 1st November 1959, ten days before the route lost its trolleybuses. *Norman Rayfield, 2RT2 Group*

L3 class 1456 from Poplar is seen at Bloomsbury at the inner London end of route 665. This class had worked the Barking Road routes since their start in June 1940 and when their work was done here they were moved on to replace older vehicles in the fleet. *C. Carter*

All is quiet at Smithfield as M1 class 1535 from West Ham depot waits for the elusive passengers at this terminus to take towards Barking on 7th June 1959. It will not be far along the route before things get busy. *Norman Rayfield, 2RT2 Group*

L3 class 1488 and its sister vehicles formed the backbone of the fleet at Poplar depot, and therefore the bulk of the everyday operation for the 665s.

North Woolwich was a busy bus and trolleybus terminus by the free ferry. The 669 shared the stand with the peak hour 569 and 685 and L3 class 1450 waits for time before returning to Aldgate. The vehicle behind is one of a small number of L3 class vehicles with sliding windows.

The familiar Burtons style shop occupies the corner plot in this view at East Street, Barking. 1482 is a chassisless L3 working the 567 to Aldgate. The local authority paid for the privilege of using the traction standard as a support for their street lighting. *Norman Rayfield, 2RT2 Group*

Stage 5
2nd/3rd February 1960
Depots: West Ham and Walthamstow.

Route 557 Liverpool Street to Chingford Mount was replaced by new 256 Moorgate to Chingford Mount and new 257 London Bridge to Chingford Mount.

Route 669 Stratford Broadway to North Woolwich was directly replaced by new bus 69. Route 238 (introduced at stage four) was also strengthened.

Route 685 Walthamstow to Silvertown and North Woolwich was replaced by new 58

The replacement of the circular services 689/690 by the 162 and 272 caused the loss of direct journeys between East Ham High Street and Barking Road but on the other hand the new bus routes provided some new extensions. The peak-hour extension of the 272 to Royal Albert Dock was short lived however. The 256 provided a new connection between north east London and Moorgate.

K2 class 1253 was a lucky survivor in the fleet. It replaced the original choice for preservation, namely 260, and took its place in the LT collection to represent the standard London trolleybus in original condition. It is working the 557 from Walthamstow in this view at Liverpool Street. Subsequently, 260 was rescued by a group of enthusiasts and is also preserved. *Norman Rayfield, 2RT2 Group*

East End rebuilding is in evidence in Plaistow Road in this mid-fifties view of E1 574 on the 669. The schedules allowed 32 minutes for the trip from North Woolwich to Stratford at a frequency of about every five minutes. *C. Carter*

A very deserted Silvertown Way with L3 1525 on route 669. The traction standards here could not be sunk the usual six feet below ground owing to the decking on which the roadway was built. The solution was to brace them with steel poles as seen here.

L3 1437 is working the shuttle service of the busy 685, a part of the route which operated from Crooked Billett to Lea Bridge Road, where it turned by way of a loop via Waterloo Road and Gloucester Road. It has just passed the Lighthouse Church in Markhouse Road. *C. Carter*

H1 class 800 operates from Walthamstow in this view of it on route 685 at Leyton Church Street about to cross Lea Bridge Road. The route linked the busy areas of Walthamstow, Leyton, Forest Gate and Upton Park, where West Ham football traffic was considerable.

The Stratford circulars of the 689 and 690 worked from Stratford Broadway to East Ham by way of a loop. The 689 worked clockwise via Plashet Grove, High Street North, Barking Road and Green Street, and the 690 in the opposite direction. M1 class 1544 from West Ham is seen at East Ham station on 10th January 1960. *Norman Rayfield, 2RT2 Group*

L3 class 1384 on the 690 is about to turn left at Green Street. It will travel along the Barking Road before turning left again down High Street North and then another left into Plashet Grove as it makes its way back to Stratford. The Boleyn would be packed with West Ham supporters at home games, the Upton Park ground being only a few hundred yards away. *C. Carter*

The Docks terminus was a hive of activity at the beginning and end of the workers' shifts, and a purpose built terminus was constructed here. H1 765 and E1 587 share the stand. *Norman Rayfield, 2RT2 Group*

Stage 6
26th/27th April 1960
Depots: West Ham and Walthamstow

Route 623 Manor House and Woodford directly replaced by new 123 extended from Woodford to Ilford.

Route 625 Winchmore Hill and Woodford replaced by new route 275 between Woodford Bridge and Enfield (Mon-Fri) Woodford Bridge and Winchmore Hill (Sats) and Woodford Bridge and Turnpike Lane (Suns).

Route 687 Walthamstow to V&A Docks replaced by revised route 41 (now Archway to Stratford Broadway) between Forest Road and Leyton and new route 278 between Chingford Mount (Wanstead Flats on Sundays) and V&A Docks.

Route 697 Chingford Mount to V&A Docks via Balaam Street directly replaced by new 249A with some Monday to Friday journeys extended from Chingford Mount to Chingford, Royal Forest Hotel. Route 69 extended on Monday to Saturday from Stratford to Chingford Mount. Walthamstow to Leyton section of 697 and 699 also covered by an extension of Monday to Saturday route 34.

Route 699 Chingford Mount to V&A Docks via Greengate Street directly replaced by new 249 with some journeys extended daily from Chingford Mount to Chingford, Royal Forest Hotel. Staff journeys on 699 replaced by night bus 299.

As a result of this stage, Forest Gate bus garage was closed. The unsatisfactory 623 and 625 terminus at Woodford was abandoned with the projection of the replacement services 123 and 275 to more useful destinations. Some of the extensions, as in some of the other stages, had their downside in buses being more affected by traffic delays on the now longer routes, e.g. the 41.

Two views of J2 class 971 from Walthamstow. In the view above, it pauses outside the Ever Ready battery factory in Ferry Lane on the 623 on 3rd January 1960. In the lower view it is pictured on the 625 in Forest Road at Standard Junction bound for Wood Green.
Norman Rayfield, 2RT2 Group

Having just passed the depot at West Ham, H1 884 crosses the busy junction with Barking Road, at the Greengate. Early morning journeys were worked on the Docks routes starting 4.36am from Walthamstow in 1956. The driver of the Hillman Californian just squeezes through the gap between the bus and the island. It is 10th January 1960. *Norman Rayfield, 2RT2 Group*

The 699 shared the stand at Chingford Mount with the 697 and 557. L3 class 1403 waits for time here before returning to the Docks via Prince Regent Lane, its counterpart 697 completing the route via Freemasons Road.

Route 623 was the first to work through the junction at the Bell, Walthamstow in October 1936. J2 980 crosses the junction in Forest Road on 24th April 1960. *Norman Rayfield, 2RT2 Group*

The Black Lion in Plaistow High Street proudly boasts that it was established in 1700! Numerically the last of the E2 class, 628 passes on the 687 on a short working to Wanstead Flats. The narrow street here was provided with single traction standards with bracket arms. *Alan Cross*

The Silvertown railway line paralleled the trolleybus route between Custom House and the Docks. L3 class 1516 is seen from the railway footbridge. *John Wills, LCCTT*

697

CHINGFORD MOUNT
CUSTOM HOUSE
STRATFORD

FXH 516

BUS STOP

At the junction of Blackhorse Lane and Forest Road on 3rd January 1960, E1 class 587 crosses Forest Road on its way to the Docks. The traction standard on the far left has a white band painted on it to remind drivers to take their foot off of the power as they pass under the feeder cables here. *Norman Rayfield, 2RT2 Group*

J2 970 pauses at the stop in Tramway Avenue Stratford on route 699. It is 10th January 1960, and in just over 3 months the route will be withdrawn. *Norman Rayfield, 2RT2 Group*

Stage 7
19th/20th July 1960
Depots: Hammersmith and Highgate

Route 611 Highgate Village to Moorgate directly replaced by new 271.

Route 626 Clapham Junction to Acton replaced by new 268 Clapham Junction to Willesden Junction and Acton (Monday to Friday peaks).

Route 628 Clapham Junction to Craven Park replaced between Clapham Junction and Harlesden Jubilee Clock by new 268. Section between Jubilee Clock and Craven Park served by 660, 662 and 666.

Route 630 West Croydon to College Park directly replaced by new 220 extended to Park Royal Stadium Mon-Fri peaks. The new route mostly ran in two sections: West Croydon – Shepherds Bush and Tooting Station – Harrow Road. Also by revised route 64 between West Croydon and Wimbledon Stadium via Tooting Broadway (replacing the 630 Summerstown journeys). The 630 night journeys were replaced by late running on the new 220.

Hammersmith depot was closed to trolleybus operation. This conversion was a fairly straightforward one, but the Hammersmith depot routes saw a Mon-Fri peak reduction in vehicles of almost 20% from 65 to 53. The 271, uniquely as a former trolleybus route, has remained unchanged since its introduction.

Like all of its L1 counterparts, 1363 was fitted with coasting and run back brakes for the steep Highgate Hill. The 611 emerged from the busy traffic of the Holloway Road and entered more leafy surroundings on its way to a specially constructed trolleybus turning point in Highgate village.

Hammersmith Broadway has always been a very busy place, and a policeman on point duty is directing the traffic in this scene before the one-way system and flyover. Hanwell's F1 class 731 is on its way to Clapham Junction on the 655 and is passing Hammersmith's F1 659, which is working the 630 up to College Park followed by a Green Line RF. The trolley traction standard on the centre island is missing its ball shaped finial. *Fred Ivey*

The substantial stone frontage of Wandsworth Town Hall provides the setting for this view on 15th May 1960, when K2 class 1332 waits on the 628 to complete its journey to Clapham Junction, followed by an RTL on route 77A. Part of the old 28 tram route, the 628 would have continued beyond Clapham Junction to Victoria if the south London scheme had been realised. *Norman Rayfield, 2RT2 Group*

The traditional barber's pole adorns the front of the shop by this bus stop in Wandsworth, Putney Bridge Road. Trolleybus 549 is a D3 vehicle on the 630, and still has a way to go before the crew can have a break at West Croydon. The date is 14th April 1959. The 630 had the longest trolleybus journey at 14.85 miles from Harrow Road to West Croydon. Its northern terminus was at the junction of Harrow Road and Scrubs Lane, and fell short of what would have been a more useful objective to serve the shopping area of Harlesden. *Norman Rayfield, 2RT2 Group*

D3 class 550, withdrawn in April 1956, stands at White City station in Wood Lane in 1953 on the 626 peak hours only route. The Hammersmith routes were heavily used when there were Fulham home matches, and the annual university boat race. *Peter Jones*

On the other side of the road from the previous view, P1 1698 passes the distinctive 1950s BBC Television Centre on its way to Craven Park at the northern end of Harlesden's shopping area. *Norman Rayfield, 2RT2 Group*

The 630 penetrated deep into south London and met the 654 at Croydon. A deviation from the main route was constructed at Garratt Lane to serve Wimbledon Stadium. It was wired via Wimbledon Road and Plough Lane to serve the venue. The special stadium journeys began from Tooting Broadway, at which terminus D2 443 is seen in the company of three RTs. *Norman Rayfield, 2RT2 Group*

The, at the time, goods only railway line to Willesden Junction is on the left in this view at Wormwood Scrubs on 24th April 1960. K1 1083 is working the 628 from Hammersmith depot. *Norman Rayfield, 2RT2 Group*

A fine assortment of cars are on show on both sides of the road at Acton on 4th April 1960. K1 1085 has just started its journey to Clapham Junction on the 626, a route which never reached its full potential that would have taken it to Borough High Street had the war not intervened. *Norman Rayfield, 2RT2 Group*

F1 743 traverses St Johns Hill and will shortly terminate at Clapham Junction. It is 15th May 1960 and the 628 will be withdrawn in two months' time. *Norman Rayfield, 2RT2 Group*

Having safely descended Highgate Hill, L1 1360 on the 611 pulls up at the stop at Archway with an RF and some RT family buses behind. This was Highgate's first route to be converted to buses. *Norman Rayfield, 2RT2 Group*

Stage eight concerned only Hanwell and its two routes. The 607 was a heavily used trunk route along the Uxbridge Road, and boasted the highest total of trolleybuses on any one route on the system.
J. H. Aston

It is 1st August 1960 and it is the last time that Hanwell will supply Bank Holiday extras from Shepherds Bush to Hampton Court. F1 712 is just leaving Hampton Court, and shows a 667 side blind. The fair seen behind the trees should do good business if the rain holds off.

Stage 8
8th/9th November 1960
Depot: Hanwell.

Route 607 Uxbridge to Shepherds Bush directly replaced by new 207. Also introduced was a new Monday to Saturday 207A running between Hayes Station and Chelsea via Shepherds Bush.

Route 655 Hanwell to Hammersmith (extended from Hanwell to Acton Vale and from Hammersmith to Clapham Junction Mon-Fri peaks) directly replaced by new 255, which operated between Acton Vale and Hammersmith on Mondays to Fridays with peak extension to Clapham Junction. On Saturdays it ran between Hanwell and Hammersmith, and on Sundays between Hanwell and Brentford.

The 207A provided a new link from the Uxbridge Road to Chelsea, supplementing the 49 for part of its length. Otherwise this was another fairly straightforward conversion. Route 607 is today an express service between Uxbridge Station and White City, short distances from the termini of the trolleybus route.

Another F1, this time 669 on the 655 at Fulham Palace Road. The route's peak extensions at each end provided the longest trolleybus round trip on the system at 29½ miles, very closely followed by the 630, which was able to claim the longest one-way journey and had a round trip distance of 29⅓ miles.

Part of the long Uxbridge Road is seen at Hayes on 21st August 1960, and F1 class 731 is heading out to Uxbridge along the dual carriageway. The centre reservation traction standards have been adapted to take the local authority street lighting. *Norman Rayfield*

Wires to and from Hanwell depot can be seen in this view taken on 21st August 1960. F1 654 picks up at the stop in the Broadway on its way to Shepherds Bush. *Norman Rayfield, 2RT2 Group*

Hanwell depot was completely rebuilt for trolleybus operation and the forecourt was used for terminating buses which accessed the depot via its side entrance in Jessamine Road. F1 665 waits on the 655 whilst F1 737 is parked up ready for a journey on the 607. *Norman Rayfield, 2RT2 Group*

F1 733 is about to turn into the stand at Uxbridge on 27th September 1959 after its long trip from Shepherds Bush on the 607. *Norman Rayfield, 2RT2 Group*

The only member of the D1 class was 384, a prototype Leyland 70-seater. It picks up a passenger here at Hayes on the 607 in the early fifties. *Fred Reynolds*

Stage 9
31st January/1st February 1961
Depot: Highgate

Routes 513/613 Hampstead Heath to Parliament Hill Fields, via Holborn, replaced by extensions to routes 39 from Camden Town to Parliament Hill Fields, 45 from Farringdon Street to Hampstead Heath and 63 from King's Cross to Parliament Hill Fields. Night journeys on 513/613 replaced by new N93 Hampstead Heath to Trafalgar Square.

Route 615 Parliament Hill Fields to Moorgate directly replaced by new 214.

Routes 517/617 North Finchley to Holborn. Replaced by new 17 North Finchley to Farringdon Street; extended to Camberwell Green on Mondays to Fridays; terminating at King's Cross on Sundays. Also route 143 (Hendon Central to Archway Station) extended to Farringdon Street on Mondays to Saturdays.

Route 639 Hampstead Heath to Moorgate directly replaced by new 239.

Route 653 Aldgate to Tottenham Court Road directly replaced by new 253 Aldgate to Tottenham Court Road.

The replacement of the 513/613 by extensions of three existing bus routes was unique in the conversion programme. The 39 extension gave Parliament Hill Fields a direct service to the West End for the first time. The extension of the 143 over the 517/617 to Farringdon Street transformed a reliable local service into a less reliable trunk route.

L3 1390 has just travelled from Highgate depot down Junction Road and Fortess Road to turn right into Fortess Walk, where it is about to join the 613 route. The journey up to this point was along roads not served by a regular trolleybus route and used only for depot runs. *Denis Battams*

RTW13 on route 24 follows J2 997 as it nears the terminus at Hampstead Heath in September 1959. The terminus was reached by way of Fleet Road, and vehicles leaving did so via Agincourt Road. This one way working followed the route previously used by trams.

It is a miserable day and if the clock is to be believed it is 1.45pm. L3 1380 has its saloon lights on as it leads K2 1243 away on their respective trips north to North Finchley and Wood Green. 1380 was the only trolleybus to bear the FXF registration mark and the K2 behind displays front posters designed to attract advertisers.

The L2 class were identical to the L1s except that they were not equipped with the coasting and runback brakes. 1370 is working the 513 to Holborn on a fine sunny day. *Transport Treasury*

The L1s were used on routes other than the intended 611, and 1360 is working the 517 in the bustling Holloway Road. It shows front adverts for the Ilford local store of Harrison Gibson. The date is 30th June 1960. *Pamlin Prints*

A short turning point was provided at Mile End Gate, using a loop via Brady Street and Darling Row. L3 class 1392 makes use of it here on the 653 on 22nd September 1960. The once fairly common 'bubble car' is represented on the left. *Denis Battams, 2RT2 Group*

Route 613 provided a link from the City to Hampstead Heath and Parliament Hill Fields in a curious U shape route. Trolleybus 954 at Holborn Circus was the first of the L2 class chassisless buses with MCCW bodywork, and could always be distinguished by the cream band below the windscreen. *Mirrorpix*

The complex junction at Manor House was used by eight trolleybus routes and it was a skilled job for drivers to negotiate. L3 1442 passes through on the 653 on its way to Hackney Station on 31st January 1961. *Norman Rayfield, 2RT2 Group*

Right K1 class 1062 spent a little time at Highgate depot early in 1960, before moving on to Wood Green and lastly Isleworth. *Michael Dryhurst*

Opposite top The grand backdrop of Kings Cross station looms large as L1 class 1362 passes on the 615. Nine trolleybus services met here, making it one of the areas most served by trolleybus routes. Many short workings used the extensive layout, turning via Swinton Street. *Denis Battams, 2RT2 Group*

Opposite This is East Finchley, and the bridges carrying the Northern Line span the Great North Road at this point. L3 class 1525 passes under on the 617 on 31st January 1961. A turn was provided here on the station forecourt for short workings. *Norman Rayfield, 2RT2 Group*

Stage 10
25th/26th April 1961
Depots: Highgate, Wood Green and Edmonton

Route 627 Waltham Cross to Tottenham Court Road directly replaced by new 127, extended from Tottenham Court Road to Victoria. South of Tottenham on Monday to Saturday it was also covered by new 276 between Tottenham and Brixton (no service south of Charing Cross on Saturdays).

Route 629 Enfield to Tottenham Court Road directly replaced by new 269.

Route 659 Waltham Cross to Holborn replaced by new 259 with the Holborn loop working abandoned, all buses approaching and leaving the Holborn terminus via Grays Inn Road. Withdrawn between Waltham Cross and Edmonton on Mon-Fri.

Route 679 Waltham Cross to Smithfield directly replaced by new 279; extended from Waltham Cross to Flamstead End on Saturdays. New Monday to Friday route 279A Flamstead End to Tottenham Hale introduced at the same time.

The 127 was usefully extended beyond the 627 terminus near the top of Tottenham Court Road, but the 269 was not. Neither route, nor the 276, was to be long-lived. The residents of Flamstead End were given a newly provided link to Waltham Cross and south.

Edmonton's P1 class 1710 travels down Upper Street, Islington on 24th April 1961. The 679 served the busy meat market at Smithfield and many early morning journeys were operated, including some from Highgate starting at 3.49am to the market. *Norman Rayfield, 2RT2 Group*

Wood Green was home to the H1 class for many years, and 886 is seen here in the mid-fifties leaving Enfield for its long trip south to the edge of the West End.

Below Another 629 view at Enfield Town, with K2 1200 starting its journey south. After it reaches Palmers Green, it will be paralleled all the way to Tottenham Court Road by the 29 bus route along a very busy traffic corridor. When replaced by bus 269, the trolleybus route kept its existing southern terminus, even though when it was introduced London Transport wanted a terminus nearer the centre.

Waltham Cross was the most northerly point reached on the system. The routes here shared the Hertford Road south as far as Seven Sisters Road, where they split to serve areas beyond Manor House and Stamford Hill. K2 class 1197 and 1242 are seen before pulling on to the stand on 24th April 1961. *Norman Rayfield, 2RT2 Group*

Tottenham Court Road is the scene as K3 1691 passes a British Railways three-wheel Scammel lorry on 14th September 1959. The 627 was one of several routes to help move the football crowds after matches at White Hart Lane when Tottenham Hotspur were playing at home. *Norman Rayfield, 2RT2 Group*

K2 1339 has left the long Hertford Road and reached Manor House. It is followed by short working K2 1335 on the 653. The 659 journey time was 65 minutes on Monday-Friday, with a service interval of six minutes in the peak hours. *Norman Rayfield, 2RT2 Group*

It was always argued that the trolleybus routes never quite reached their desired objective, and Tottenham Court Road was an example. They were tucked away from the main shopping area by way of a loop, and any shoppers wanting Oxford Street would have to walk south or get a bus to complete their journey. Howland Street formed part of the turning loop at Tottenham Court Road and J3 class 1045 is northbound for Waltham Cross on 14th September 1959. *Norman Rayfield, 2RT2 Group*

Stage 11
18th/19th July 1961
Depots: Edmonton and Stamford Hill

The 543/643 routes linked
Wood Green with Holborn,
and also had an all-night
variant that worked from
Stamford Hill. This view at
Holborn Circus was taken on
26th April 1961 and shows
K2 1224. *Norman Rayfield,
2RT2 Group*

Route 543 Wood Green to Holborn loop (via Grays Inn Road) directly replaced by new 243. Night journeys replaced by N83 Stamford Hill to Trafalgar Square.

Route 643 Wood Green to Holborn loop (via Farringdon Road) withdrawn.

Route 647 Stamford Hill to London Docks replaced by new 67 on Mondays to Saturdays; extended from Stamford Hill to Northumberland Park. On Sundays the route was directly replaced by new 243A Wood Green to London Docks, which also absorbed the 649A.

Route 649 Waltham Cross to Liverpool Street directly replaced by new 149, extended to Victoria on Mondays to Fridays.

Route 649A Wood Green to Liverpool Street replaced together with 647 by new Sunday route 243A, but diverted at Great Eastern Street to run to the Docks. Route 47 extended from Shoreditch Church to Stoke Newington.

The projection of the 647's replacement gave Northumberland Park a new link to Tottenham and Stamford Hill southwards and provided a service along Lansdowne Road for the first time. The link between Liverpool Street and Victoria provided by the 149 was also new.

164

K1 class 1112 passes through Stamford Hill on the 643. The wires leading off to the depot can be seen in the distance on the right. The trolleybus has travelled along Lordship Lane and through Tottenham to reach this point, and will now negotiate the road to Shoreditch and turn right towards Holborn.

The Old Street area has now changed almost beyond recognition. K2 class 1229 works its way along towards Holborn on the 543 on 26th April 1961. *Norman Rayfield, 2RT2 Group*

The impressive Bishopsgate Goods Yard forms the background for this view taken on 9th July 1961. K1 1151 is not far from its Liverpool Street terminus and its driver has set the blind ready for the trip back through Shoreditch and Dalston on its way north to Wood Green. Although a Sunday only route, an impressive headway of 6-8 minutes was maintained. *Denis Battams, 2RT2 Group*

K2 1233 on the 649 has just passed under the railway bridge at South Tottenham. This main road was dominated by trolleybus routes and the 76 was the only bus route to share this section of operation. South Tottenham station is today part of the London Overground network on the Gospel Oak to Barking line. The front adverts on 1233 for the 'new' Sunday Telegraph tell us that this photo was taken after February 1961. *Mick Webber collection*

The 647 terminated at London Docks, and in Dock Street are K2s 1206 and 1205 on 9th July 1961. Like all of the routes that served the Docks, there were early morning special journeys, the first one from Stamford Hill being at 4.50am in 1957. *Denis Battams, 2RT2 Group*

K2 1234 works the 649 on 9th July 1961 and is seen at Dalston Junction. The operations on the Hertford Road routes were intense; many journeys were scheduled to turn at Ponders End, where they terminated on the forecourt of Enfield bus garage, and others were turned short there. This involved a short detour off the main route, along Southbury Road. Many extras were worked on the Hertford Road services when Spurs were playing at home. *Denis Battams, 2RT2 Group*

Liverpool Street was the terminus for three trolleybus routes, including the Sunday-only 649A – the only post-war trolleybus route with a suffix letter. K2 1229 is seen here at the head of a line-up that includes a portent to the future in the shape of a Routemaster on the 257. The date is 16th July 1961. *Norman Rayfield, 2RT2 Group*

Stage 12
7th/8th November 1961

Depots: Wood Green and Finchley.

Routes 521/621 North Finchley to Holborn. Replaced by new 221 North Finchley to Farringdon Street and route 168 extended on Mondays to Saturdays from Farringdon Street via Grays Inn Road, Holloway and Finsbury Park to Turnpike Lane.

Route 609 Barnet to Moorgate directly replaced by new 104.

Route 641 Winchmore Hill to Moorgate directly replaced by new 141; extended from Moorgate to Grove Park on Mondays to Fridays.

The 104 saw the first use of RMLs and the only use of them during the replacement of trolleybuses. Despite their seating capacity being only two more than the 70-seater trolleybuses they replaced, the number of vehicles allocated to the route on Mon-Fri was savagely cut from 26 to 19. The extension of the 141 was of such a length that it was operated in sections.

M1 class 1540 from Finchley has just pulled out of Bounds Green Road, and leaves behind the more affluent area of New Southgate. It will descend Jolly Butchers Hill and pass Wood Green depot before travelling on to turn short at Kings Cross. *Terry Cooper Collection/Mick Webber*

Turnpike Lane was and still is a very busy interchange point between the Piccadilly Line and local buses. The bus station here was also wired for short workings. L3 1520 glides past on a sunny day on its way south to Holborn.

The large junction at Manor House had more than 300 through trolleybuses per hour in 1958 plus a further 18 terminating vehicles during the height of the peak running period. Finchley's L3 1476 pauses on the 621 with a once familiar Evening Standard newspaper delivery van behind. *John Aldridge Collection*

M1 class 1540 turns into Seven Sisters Road at the Nags Head on a short working of route 521. The Nags Head was host to eleven routes with a peak of nearly 300 vehicles per hour passing through. It is a dismal day, and a lone policeman stands on point duty on the left whilst a new Routemaster takes the lead on the 279. *Terry Cooper Collection/Mick Webber*

The weather looks awful in this view of 1370 at Nags Head as the L2 makes its way towards Barnet followed by an RTW. The 609 followed a very straight route from its northern terminus, through Archway and down the Holloway Road before going off towards Islington on its journey south to the City, where it turned amongst the offices at Finsbury Square. *Terry Cooper Collection/Mick Webber*

Upper Street Islington, at Islington Green, with L3 1518 followed by an RT on route 19. The bustling area of the Angel and the City Road have been left behind, and soon the route will fork off to the left at Highbury and follow the Holloway Road.

Wood Green finally lost its trolleybuses when route 641 was withdrawn. The H1 class was strongly linked to this depot, and 757 in Wood Green High Road works the route in this view. The 641 started at Winchmore Hill and made its way through the suburban Palmers Green before joining other routes at Wood Green to continue south to Finsbury Square.

Stage 13
2nd/3rd January 1962
Depots: Colindale, Finchley and Stonebridge.

Route 645 Barnet to Canons Park replaced by new 245 running between Stanmore Station and North Finchley and new 260 on the section between North Finchley and Barnet. Route 2 extended from Golders Green to North Finchley.

Route 660 North Finchley to Hammersmith replaced by new 260 running between Barnet and Willesden Junction (or Hammersmith in Mon-Fri peaks and on Sats).

Route 660 Acton Vale to Paddington Green Mon-Fri morning peak journeys directly replaced by new 293, with Mon-Fri afternoon peak journeys added.

Route 662 Sudbury to Paddington Green replaced by route 18 on which the Edgware to London Bridge Sunday service became daily.

Route 666 Edgware to Hammersmith directly replaced by new 266.

Both the 645 and 666 had extensions to more useful termini when replaced by buses. At the same time as this conversion, new route 292 replaced the 52A between Borehamwood and Colindale and continued on to Willesden Garage over trolleybus routes 660 and 666. The Sudbury terminus was eliminated by what was in effect an extension of the 662 to Harrow and Edgware under the number 18. Colindale depot was closed.

Stage 13 will always be remembered for the heavy snow that fell before the conversion. N1 class 1586 from Colindale depot struggles along Ballards Lane Finchley, on its way to Barnet. *Terry Cooper Collection/Mick Webber*

Harlesden, Jubilee Clock, was the meeting point of routes 626, 628, 660, 662, 664 and 666. N2 1648 has taken the right hand wire to take it away from the High Street to travel down Old Oak Lane and serve the industrial area of North Acton. *C. Carter*

Routes 660, 664 and 666 parted company with the 662 here at Craven Park where it took the left wire towards Stonebridge, Wembley and Sudbury. C3 286 is seen on 28th February 1959. *Norman Rayfield, 2RT2 Group*

Hammersmith Grove was the stand for the 660, 666, 667 and many 655s. M1 class 1547 is operating from Finchley on the 660. The route shared the wires with the 666 as far as Cricklewood Broadway, where the two parted company; the 660 for North Finchley and the 666 for Edgware. *Terry Cooper Collection/Mick Webber*

The 662 followed the Harrow Road from Paddington Green to Sudbury. Many unnumbered extras operated when events at Wembley Stadium dictated, and a stand at Wembley Hill Road was used for that purpose. N1 1641 is the vehicle in this view at Harlesden.

L3 1465 works the 645 on 6th August 1961 at Cricklewood Broadway. The 645 took a 'V' shape 63-minute route between Canons Park and Barnet, although the two termini were only just over three miles apart as the crow flies. *Norman Rayfield, 2RT2 Group*

Stonebridge depot was dominated in later years by the N class vehicles that had arrived from east London. The 662 is represented here by N2 1665 and N1 1641. The location is College Park, at the junction of Harrow Road and Scrubs Lane, and the junction wires for the latter can be seen in the distance. Some 662s turned short here.

Stage 14
8th/9th May 1962

Depots: Fulwell and Isleworth.

Route 601 Tolworth to Twickenham directly replaced by new 281.

Route 602 The Dittons to Kingston loop directly replaced by new 282.

Route 603 Tolworth to Kingston loop directly replaced on Mondays to Saturdays by new 283. Sunday service replaced by 281 between Kingston and Tolworth and two-way working around the Kingston loop on this day by new 282.

Route 604 Wimbledon to Hampton Court replaced by extension of route 131 (Walton-on-Thames to Kingston) to Wimbledon.

Route 605 Wimbledon to Teddington (Twickenham on Sundays) replaced by new 285; extended from Teddington to London Airport and in Wimbledon from the station to Haydons Road. Sunday extension to Twickenham covered by new 281.

Route 657 Hounslow to Shepherds Bush replaced by extensions of routes 117 (Egham to Hounslow, Mon-Sat) and 81B (London Airport to Hounslow, Sundays) to Shepherds Bush. Route 116 also extended from Hounslow to Turnham Green (Mon-Fri) and Hammersmith (Mon-Fri peaks and Sats).

Route 667 Hammersmith to Hampton Court directly replaced by new 267.

Bus routes 116, 117 and 131, and the 81B on Sundays, gained lengthy extensions with the final conversion. One trolleybus replacement route, the 285, also went a long way beyond its former terminus to serve the increasingly busy Heathrow Airport. The 117 was worked in sections on Mon-Fri, travelling its full length being possible only on Saturdays. The first and last conversions seem to have had the most complaints from the public, those for this last one being about the less reliable running of the longer routes, frequency reductions and the removal of some bus stops and resiting of others, which probably happened more with this stage than any other. Isleworth depot was closed.

The Kingston loop routes were something of a backwater on the London trolleybus network and L3 1483 is seen at Surbiton on 25th March 1962. It would travel on through the suburb to Tolworth where it turned and stood by a triangular green opposite the Red Lion. *Norman Rayfield, 2RT2 Group*

L3 class 1472 was one of six of the class fitted with sliding ventilators instead of the usual half drop. On Sundays the 605 was extended from its Mon-Sat terminus at Teddington to Twickenham, which it shared with the 601. *Norman Rayfield, 2RT2 Group*

The Kingston local routes worked a loop via Richmond Road, Park Road and Kings Road, the 602 anti-clockwise and the 603 clockwise. L3 1464 is on its way to the Dittons, the most lightly used of the London trolleybus termini. *Terry Cooper Collection/Mick Webber*

Fulwell's link with the rest of the system was the 667. It met other major routes at Hammersmith, and was a popular means of getting to Hampton Court at weekends and Bank Holidays. Signs of the old LUT tram track can be seen here at Twickenham on 8th May 1962 as L3 1393 makes for Hampton Court. *Norman Rayfield, 2RT2 Group*

Isleworth operated only one route, the 657, which linked Shepherds Bush with Hounslow. It shared the road with the 667 between Youngs Corner and Busch Corner, and at the end was worked exclusively by the K class Leylands. On 22nd April 1962, K1 1144 is nearing the end of its journey in Hounslow. *Norman Rayfield, 2RT2 Group*

L3 1430 passes through Kingston en-route for Twickenham. In the opposite direction, the 601 turned right for Surbiton and Tolworth, where it traversed an anti-clockwise loop via Ewell Road, a road running parallel to the Kingston by pass, and Warren Drive, where trolleybuses on the route stood. *Terry Cooper Collection/Mick Webber*

Kings Road is on the Kingston loop, and L3 1512 works the 602 on 25th March 1962. The 'fairy lights' between the wires can be seen in the distance, fitted to help drivers maintain the correct driving line on curves after dark or in foggy conditions. *Norman Rayfield, 2RT2 Group*

The 604 was a busy link between Hampton Court and Wimbledon via Kingston, New Malden and Raynes Park. The stretch of Kingston Road from New Malden into Kingston was exclusive to the trolleybuses. L3 1504 travels through Raynes Park on 18th March 1962. *Norman Rayfield, 2RT2 Group.*

When the author boarded 1521 at Hampton Court, all was relatively quiet, there were even seats to spare. The journey got underway, and gradually as it went through Kingston, a procession of cars began to follow. This built up all the way to Wimbledon, where there was a large crowd waiting to greet the trolleybus. As the journey progressed back towards Kingston, small crowds gathered at Raynes Park and Malden, and people waved from their front gates. This scene is near the end of the trip at Hampton. The final yards of the journey were led to the depot by busmen with lighted flares. *Bernard King*

The crowds of people wait at Fulwell depot for the arrival of 1521, and the closure of the London system. The overhead glints in the street lights, and it will not be too long before the power is switched off. *Bernard King*

In the days leading up to 8th May, a private film crew had been at work filming at the depot and locally. They filmed the events during the last day, and the trip around the Kingston loop by Diddler No.1, and they were in place in the early hours of 9th May to record the last arrival. The gathered crowds are at the depot gates, and the film cameras are on the tower wagon ready for 1521 to appear. *Terry Cooper Collection/ Mick Webber*

Below 1521 safely enters the depot gates, carefully making its way through the throng of people. Balloons and flags are tied to the booms and finally the largest trolleybus system in the world has come to an end. *Bernard King*

Left The hand-held newspaper placard says it all. *Mike Beamish*

SERVING LONDON TROLLEYBUSES

With an organisation as large as London Transport, a substantial fleet of service vehicles was required. The trolleybus fleet had its own special maintenance vehicles within this fleet. In the early days, former buses were converted to tower wagons to join the fleet of tramway towers already in service. These were followed by purpose-built new tower wagons, along with pole carriers, and a fleet of breakdown tenders. In the years leading up to the changeover to buses, newer vehicles were bought to assist with the conversion programme

Many depots had their own tower wagons and breakdown tenders, and there were also a few dedicated tower wagon sheds around the system. The tower wagons and breakdown tenders were painted red, and the pole carrier lorries in Brunswick green.

Sandwiched between two trolleybuses is 101N. This AEC Monarch tower wagon was new in 1938 and is seen here with its crew working on the overhead. It was supplied with 100N and the two lasted until 1961. They were originally numbered E26 and E27 and this one was normally based at Highgate.

28H began life as NS1240 and was converted in 1936 to a tower wagon along with eight others of its class. The crew here attend to a feeder wire.
David Packer

Above 95Q was one of six AEC Mercury pole carriers supplied in November 1936. It is posed at Fulwell, when new, demonstrating the art of lifting a pole. It outlasted the trolleybus system, being withdrawn in October 1963, and was latterly based at Finchley. *LT Museum*

The six AEC Mercury vehicles supplied in 1936 were followed in 1937 by three AEC Monarchs. The Mercury shown here is 91Q, which survived until 1959. *Alan Cross*

In 1958, London Transport bought five new AEC Mercury tower wagons for use with the dismantling of the system. 1076Q was one of these, and in this view the crew and their vehicle will soon have to make room for L3 1444 which is approaching. This tower wagon was sold to Reading Corporation in 1964. *John Shearman*

A constable looks on as 83Q and its crew take down wires in Kingston. This tower wagon was sold to George Cohen, the contractor paid to dismantle the system, in January 1962. *Terry Cooper Collection/Mick Webber*

An unidentified AEC Mercury tower wagon is working here on Kingston Bridge. The last 601, 604 and 605s have gone, and the wires are being cut down. *Terry Cooper Collection/Mick Webber*

The Board bought nineteen breakdown tenders. Twelve were Albions and seven Leylands. They were supplied between 1937 and 1939, and most lasted until the end of the system. 122A from Lea Bridge is one of the Albion variety, and is tending to the needs of K2 class 1191. *Mick Webber Collection*

LONDON TROLLEYBUSES AT NIGHT

A trolleybus at night had a certain warmth to it. The reflection of the street lights on the overhead, and the silent approach and warm yellow glow, was somehow reassuring. There were just a handful of trolleybus routes that ran in the middle of the night. The 1950 map shows just five. The 513/613 between Holborn and Hampstead, the 543/643 between Stamford Hill and Holborn, the 612 from Mitcham to Battersea, the 628 from Hammersmith to Clapham Junction and the 665 between Poplar and Bloomsbury. These routes were not numbered until 18/19th June 1946, running unnumbered until then like their tram counterparts.

In addition to these routes, there were numerous night staff journeys operated by most depots, and because a conductor was carried to operate the frogs, members of the public could be carried. Timetables of these workings were not available to the public.

This short chapter illustrates normal daytime routes after dark in an attempt to show the special magic of trolleybuses at night-time. Most of the photographs were taken on the last nights of operation.

Left All is quiet at Holborn. K2 1326 waits for time to return to Stamford Hill depot on the last 643. Shiny new Routemasters will be ready to roll out on the replacement 243 the next day. *Terry Cooper Collection/ Mick Webber*

Above right The Tottenham Court Road stand is deserted on 27th January 1961, with just four more days of trolleybus operation left on the 653. L1 class 1369 waits for a trip to Stamford Hill. *Denis Battams, 2RT2 Group*

Right K1 class 1062 waits at Shoreditch Church on a short working of the 557. It is 2nd February 1960, and it is the last night of operation. RMs will take over in the morning. *Denis Battams, 2RT2 Group*

Above Trolleybuses stood on the wrong side of the road at Bloomsbury Red Lion Square, and L3 class 1453 waits here on the 665. It is the last night of operation, 10th November 1959, and for the first time in the conversion scheme, Routemasters will replace trolleybuses the following day. *Denis Battams, 2RT2 Group*

Left A last night, and the last 613 is ready to leave Hampstead Heath. L1 1360 will make its way back to Highgate depot on 31st January 1961 and the route will pass into history. *Denis Battams, 2RT2 Group*

Above right The London Docks lost its trolleybus service on 18th July 1961. K1 class 1135 is seen on the last night with 'the last 647' chalked on the front dash. *Terry Cooper Collection/Mick Webber*

Right Wood Green's last trolleybus was K2 1353. Crammed full with staff, it makes its way to the depot in the early hours of 8th November 1961. *Terry Cooper Collection/ Mick Webber*

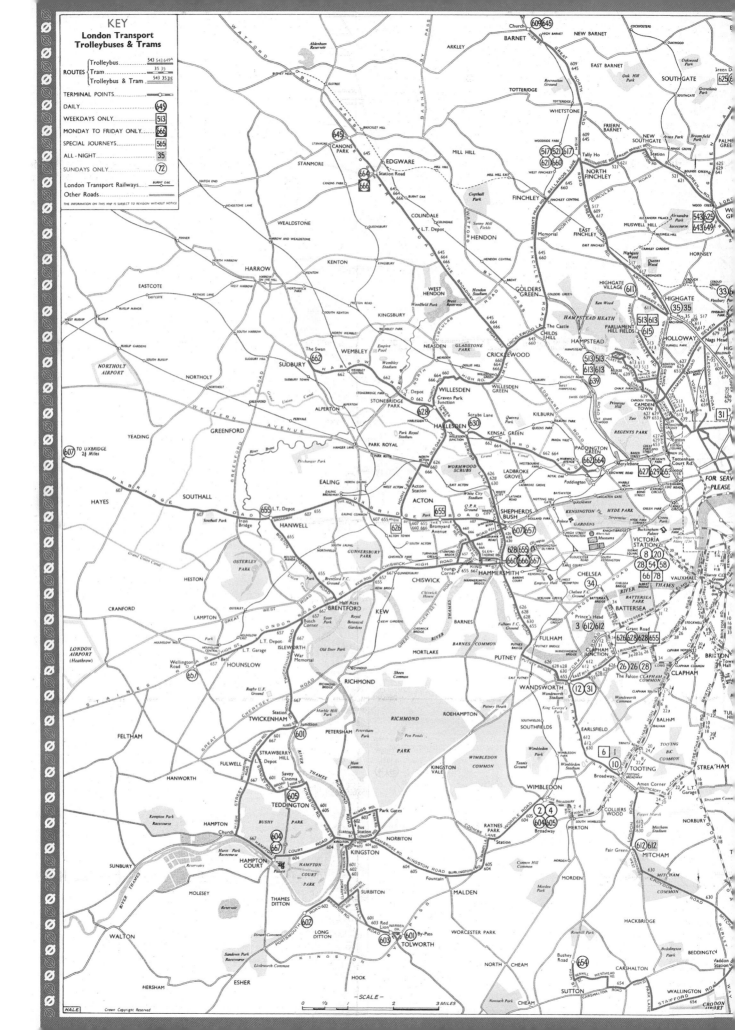

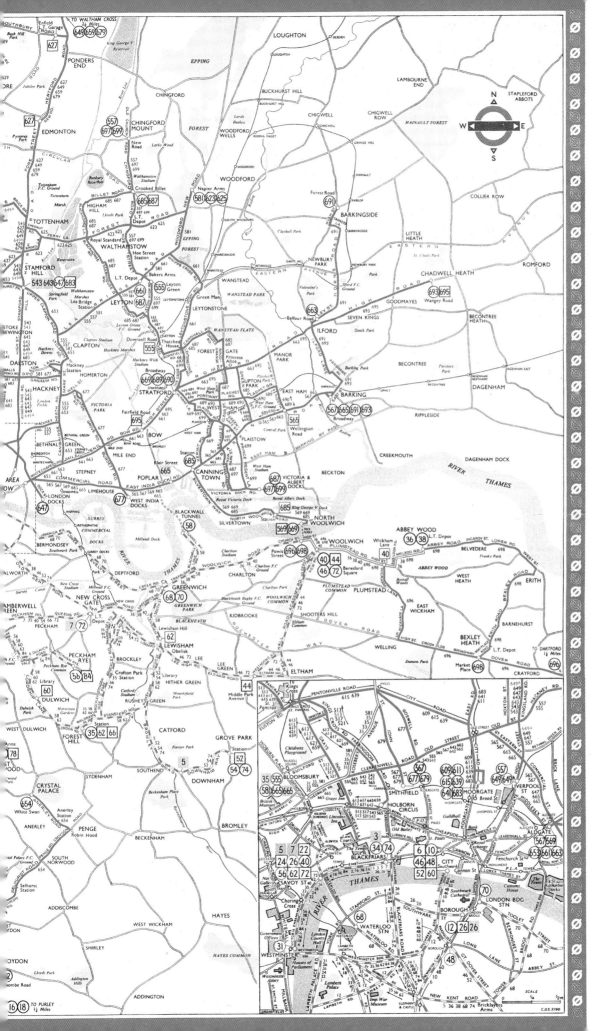

The free-issue
London trolleybus
and tram map
showing the systems
at January 1950.

193

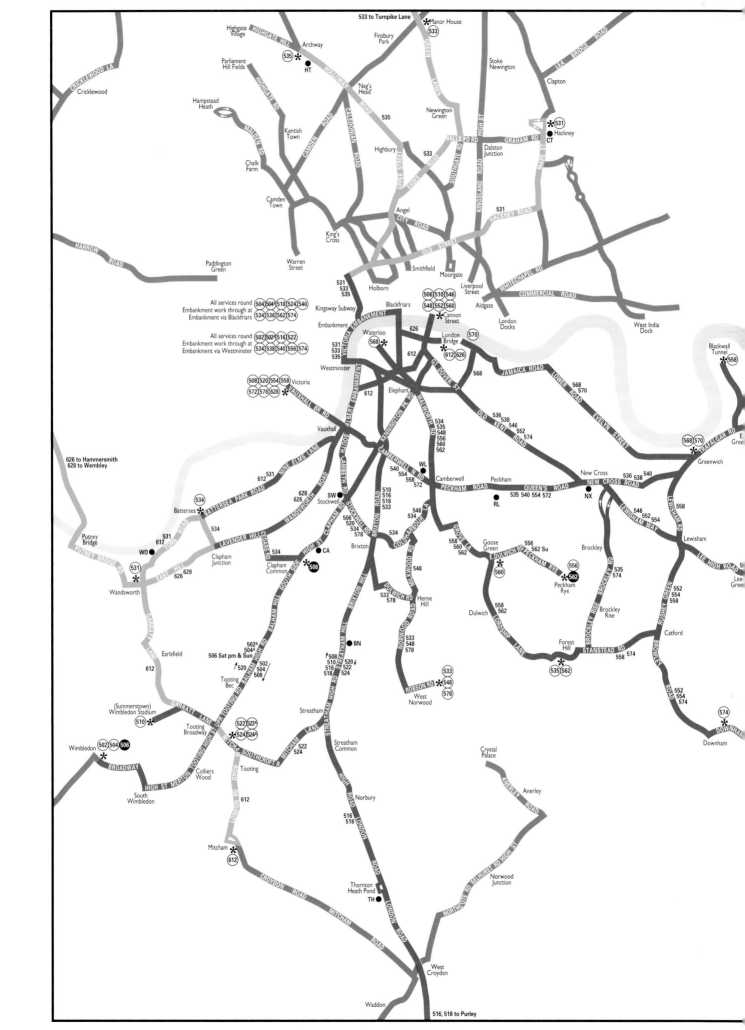

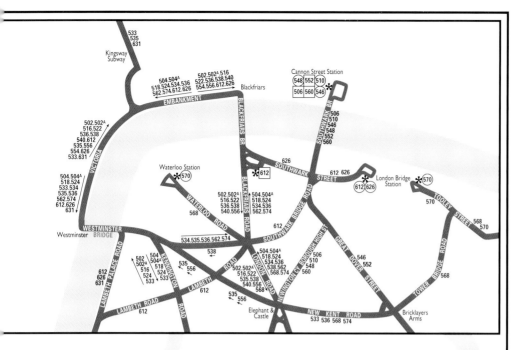

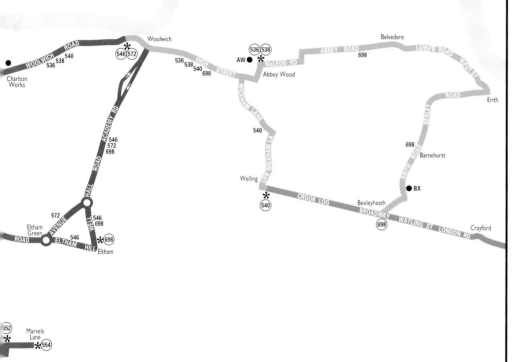

The abandonment of the south London tram to trolleybus programme following the second world war robbed London of an extended area of trolleybus operation. Buses took over these routes between 1950 and 1952 instead. Various estimates have appeared of the number of extra trolleybuses that would have been needed for south London but the increase in the fleet would have been at least 50%. New or converted depots would have been brought into use at Abbey Wood, Brixton, Camberwell, Clapham, New Cross, Rye Lane, Stockwell and Thornton Heath. Wandsworth depot would have become all-trolleybus. New turning circles would also have been needed, not all of which had been finalised at the start of the war. In some cases, short extensions beyond the tram terminus would have been made to reach a suitable turn or, as at Grove Park, to provide extra terminus capacity. Depot codes were not used during the period of the south London planning, but in the map we have used the codes that were later employed for the bus garages that stood on the same site. This map shows what was planned at the time the Second World War started. Route 612, following the operation of tram route 12, had a planned night service that differed from the day service, diverging from the day route at the junction of Lambeth Road and Lambeth Palace Road to run over Westminster Bridge and Victoria Embankment to terminate at the western end of Southwark Street. The south London plans were slightly revised after the war, before the tram to trolleybus scheme was abandoned.

South London Proposals

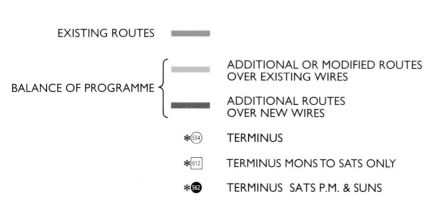

Drawn by Mike Harris

195

APPENDIX 1: THE DEVELOPMENT OF THE CONVERSION PROGRAMME

June 1954

			Depots	Scheduled Trolleybuses
1	January 1958	654, 696, 698	BX, CN	106
2	April 1958	565, 567, 569, 665	PR, WH	100
3	July 1958	669, 685, 689, 690	WW, WH	93
4	October 1958	687, 697, 699	WW, WH	80
5	January 1959	557, 611, 623, 625	WW, HT	77
6	April 1959	555, 581, 677	CT, LB	98
7	July 1959	661, 663, 695	BW	96
8	January 1960	513/613, 615, 639, 653	HT	118
9	April 1960	627, 659, 679	HT, EM	101
10	July 1960	543/643, 647, 649, 683	EM, SF	110
11	October 1960	629, 641	WN	96
12	April 1961	521/621, 609, 645, 660	CE, FY, SE	119
13	July 1961	662, 664, 666, 691, 693	CE, SE, ID	115
14	October 1961	607, 655	HL	108
15	January 1962	626, 628, 630	HB	74

November 1954

	1955	654, 696, 698	CN, BX	112
1	January 1958	555, 581, 677	CT, LB	91
2	April 1958	661, 663, 695	BW, ID	89
3	July 1958	565, 567, 569, 665	PR, WH	97
4	January 1959	557, 669, 685, 689, 690	WW, WH	110
5	April 1959	623, 625, 687, 697, 699	WW, WH	102
6	July 1959	611, 626, 628, 630	HB, HT, SE	84
7	October 1959	607, 655	HL	100
8	April 1960	513/613, 517/617, 615, 639, 653	HT	110
9	July 1960	627, 659, 679	EM, HT, WN	105
10	October 1960	543/643, 647, 649, 683	EM, SF	99
11	January 1961	629, 641	WN	82
12	April 1961	521/621, 609, 645, 660	CE, FY, SE	116
13	July 1961	662, 664, 666, 691, 693	CE, SE, ID	100

December 1955

1	January 1959	654, 696, 698	CN, BX	95
2	April 1959	555, 581, 677	CT, LB	91
3	July 1959	661, 663, 695	BW, ID	85
4	October 1959	565, 567, 569, 665	PR, WH	92
5	January 1960	557, 669, 685, 689, 690	WW, WH	103
6	May 1960	623, 625, 687, 697, 699	WW, WH	107
7	August 1960	611, 626, 628, 630	HT, HB	82
8	November 1960	607, 655	HL	100
9	March 1961	513/613, 517/617, 615, 639, 653	HT	109
10	June 1961	627, 659, 679	EM, SF	105
11	September 1961	543/643, 647, 649, 683	EM, SF	99
12	December 1961	629, 641	WN	82
13	April 1962	521/621, 609, 645, 660	CE, FY, SE	110
14	July 1962	662, 664, 666, 691, 693	CE, SE, ID	106

September 1958 (No figures given for scheduled trolleybuses)

1	1 March 1959	654, 696, 698	CN, BX
2	26 April 1959	555, 581, 677	CT, LB
3	19 July 1959	661, 663, 691, 693	BW, ID
4	8 November 1959	567, 569, 665	PR, WH
5	2 February 1960	557, 669, 685, 689, 690	WH, WW
6	28 April 1960	623, 625, 687, 697, 699	WH, WW, WN
7	17 July 1960	611, 626, 628, 630	HB, HT
8	6 November 1960	607, 655	HL
9	29 January 1961	513/613, 517/617, 615, 639, 653	HT
10	23 April 1961	627, 659, 679	HT, EM
11	16 July 1961	543/643, 647, 649	EM, SF
12	5 November 1961	521/621, 629, 641	WN, FY
13	28 January 1962	609, 645, 660, 662, 666	SE, FY, CE

LB, ID, IH, HB and CE depots closed

INDEX